Bill Jones and Chris Williams

B. L. COOMBES

University of Wales Press

Cardiff 1999

SOUTH

It

I

I was fascinated by that light in the sky. Night after night I watched it reddening the shadows beyond the Brecknock Beacons, sometimes fading until it only showed faintly, then brightening until it seemed that all the country was ablaze.

The winter wind that rushed across the Herefordshire fields where the swedes rotted in heaps, and carried that smell of decay into the small farmhouse which was my home, seemed to encourage the burning, until the night sky would redden still more. Sometimes I felt sure that I could see these flames and feel their warmth, but it could only have been fancy, for they were more than sixty miles away from us.

Thus B. L. Coombes began his THESE POOR HANDS: THE AUTOBIOGRAPHY OF A MINER WORKING IN SOUTH WALES (1939). In these initial paragraphs he constructed an image of himself as a young, rural Englishman, lured from his native county and its stagnant agricultural economy by the pulsating promise of the valleys of south Wales, with their industries of iron, steel and coal.

Whether or not it was possible to see the glow of the Bessemer works at Dowlais from the village of Madley in Herefordshire, where the adolescent Coombes lived with his mother and father, is hardly important. For dramatic effect Coombes may well have sought to recreate the *glow on all sides in the heaven* found by his hero George Borrow, when that famous pedestrian approached the iron town of Merthyr Tydfil at night (WILD WALES, 1862). What is more significant is that, for reasons literary, personal or both, in opening THESE POOR HANDS with this clutch of contrasts (rural/urban, agricultural/industrial, English/Welsh), Coombes deliberately simplified the complexities of his early life and experience.

B. L. Coombes, the name he used in all his published work, was born Bertie Louis Coombs Griffiths, in Wolverhampton, Staffordshire, on 9 January 1893. He was the first, and only, child of James Coombs Griffiths, at that time a grocer, and of Harriett Thompson. The details of Coombes's early life are unclear, and nowhere in his writings does he shed much light on his parents, or on his relations with them. His father *was alert, active, always hurrying to do something, but was handicapped by the limp caused by a horse falling on him during the South African War* (THESE POOR HANDS). His mother had been *slender and quite good looking in those days when he had trotted alongside and made attempts to help her in the tasks of that country home,* but *she had gone wrinkled and bent before she should have because she had worked too hard and gone without so many things she needed* ('Better Off', LEFT REVIEW, 3, No. 14, March 1938). She ended her life an impoverished widow, her son struggling to raise his own family, two counties away but a world apart, against the depressed economic climate of the inter-war years.

It is likely that Coombes's parents, who came to use the surname Cumbs, Cumbes or Coombes rather than Griffiths, had either roots or connections in the Madley district of Herefordshire, for their son regularly referred to it as their, and his, 'homeland'. Yet what Coombes did not explain in THESE POOR HANDS was that, by the time he considered leaving *the flat, rich lands* for *the barren hills,* his acquaintance with the South Wales Coalfield had been much more intimate than he led his readers to believe. As he explained in his second, unpublished autobiography, 'Home on the Hill' (1959):

I knew the smell and sound of mining as a boy. I had watched the crowds of coal grimed men coming home and had failed to recognise my own father when he was in pit clothes. I had seen many carried to their homes, and had sat up in bed many nights to watch the glowworm-like crowding of tiny lights near the pit top as the men waited to go down.

By the time Coombes was around ten years old, he was living in a terraced house in Treharris, Glamorgan, whilst his father and uncles worked, along with over 1,500 other colliers, at the local Deep Navigation Colliery. His schooling, up to the age of twelve, took place in this mining town, and the young Coombes showed some signs of literary and intellectual promise, winning a school prize for a poem written on the subject of the nearby River Taff. Yet:

After getting near the highest mark in the Scholarship . . . I rejected the schoolmaster's advice and urged my parents to carry out the ambition which I had so often heard them talk about in the evenings. A small farm was vacant and they returned to their native area in Herefordshire.
(NEATH GUARDIAN, 11 October 1963)

This move took place in either 1905 or 1906, Coombes's father obtaining the tenancy of Blenheim

3

Farm, Madley, and Coombes himself beginning work on the land as a labourer, both on the family farm and on neighbouring estates. He learned to plough, hedge, thatch and milk, to handle horses, and to appreciate the cider that was made and kept in the adjoining barn. He grew to *love the land, the seasons and the continual work that goes with them*, and *in summer, all our surroundings were lovely*. But as he explained in THE LIFE WE WANT (1944):

it was not always summer, and we could not live and have our being on surroundings alone. Life for the small man who had to depend on the land for a living was heavily handicapped. My parents worked hard. They set no limits to their efforts. But money was always scarce and the heavy rent was an ogre that shadowed all the days of our life.

The tenancy was expensive, and the land that came with it scattered *small patches of ground*. Apples and swedes were picked only to fetch pitifully low prices in the markets, and the price of coal was *too dear for us to buy*. The relatives that remained in south Wales wrote, remarkably it seemed, telling of quite the opposite situation there, where coal was plentiful and fresh produce costly. With little money coming in, *new clothes were very rare, and pocket-money was something to imagine*. The temptation to leave the land was strong, for *this*, wrote Coombes in THESE POOR HANDS, *did not suit my ideas of life. I wanted good clothes, money to spend, to see fresh places and faces, and – well, many things*. In THE LIFE WE WANT he summed up his growing sense of bitterness, *a sort of confused frustration and helplessness*:

Here we were, working hard to produce good things from the earth and to sell them, my parents urgently needing the money to bring up our small family to be good and decent citizens who in turn could enrich our country and their fellow-beings; yet there seemed no way of getting a fair price for our stuff. Around us was some of the richest and most beautiful land in the world, yet it held no encouragement or security for me and my generation.

Coombes's departure from Herefordshire was delayed, for one year (1909), by a job he found as a groom, working for a doctor in a neighbouring village. Living in, he made friends with Helen, a twenty-year-old maid and recently widowed miner's daughter, who hailed from Ammanford, Carmarthenshire. His horizons were broadened by his groom's duties (*we travelled daily, and often nightly, along the roads outside Hereford and up the Golden Valley*), visiting farms, mansions and the local workhouse, but:

I was growing towards manhood, and any talk of danger attracted me: but the main thing was that it seemed to me that in the mining areas there must be comfort and good pay.

Two of his neighbours in Madley, *time-expired soldiers*, recommended the Army as an escape from the privilege and snobbery of rural society. When Coombes showed little interest in this, ex-Hussar George 'Tiger' Jones observed

then up there in the works is the place for a young feller. Shorter hours and good money, not like as it be hereabouts – gotter graft all the hours as God sends. Ain't got to call no manner of man sir up there – no, yuh ain't.

(THESE POOR HANDS)

Coombes had a choice of destinations: relatives still in

Treharris, and also some in Maerdy in the Rhondda Fach; Helen's family in Ammanford; the doctor's brother in Cardiff; and a friend, Jack Preece, who had already left Madley for the collieries of the Vale of Neath. Putting slips of paper in the bowler hat he wore as a groom, he drew out the Vale of Neath. One day in 1910, en route to Hereford and the railway station, he took his leave of his parents and of the countryside:

I looked back from the turn at the old home and heard the dog barking his sorrow at the parting. I carried the smell of the wood fire with me, and it has hung in my senses ever since. Little things like the thud of a falling apple, the crackle of corn being handled, the smell of manure drying on a warm day, the hoot of the owl from the orchard at night, and the smell of the new bread when my mother drew it from the stone oven on a long wooden ladle, are still very sweet to me. Every year the smell of drying grass makes me crave for the hayfields, but I have never since worked in them or been in my native place for anything more than a short visit.

Coombes's destination was Resolven ('Treclewyd' in THESE POOR HANDS) in the heart of the Vale of Neath: *a wide valley shut in by splendid mountains*, and *only the width of a mountain* from *the light in the sky I had watched so much*. This was a coal-mining area: one-third of the adult male population of Glamorgan was occupied in that industry in 1911, and by the census of 1921 over half of the men in the Neath Rural District (including Resolven) were so employed. Yet, as Coombes noted, it was quite different both from the Treharris in which he had spent part of his childhood, and from the mining settlements of the Cynon and Rhondda Valleys in the central coalfield. The Vale of Neath marked the easternmost edge of the anthracite coalfield, and exhibited significant differences in both mining and settlement patterns.

Anthracite coal, suitable for use in specialized stoves, accounted for approximately 22 per cent of coal reserves in south Wales, and was, at the time of Coombes's arrival, yet to peak in terms of production and manpower (it did so in 1934). In contrast, steam coal (48 per cent of total reserves, suitable for raising steam in boilers) and bituminous coal (30 per cent, appropriate to household purposes and often known as 'house' coal), generally found in the central and eastern coalfield, were rapidly reaching their economic climax, and the inter-war years would see their decline. (Coombes was to work in seams containing all these types of coal.) Anthracite mines (often levels or drifts rather than deep-mined pits), for geological reasons, tended to be smaller than those producing steam or house coal, and because they did not attract thousands of workers, the mining settlements that clustered around them also remained comparatively modest. Thus it was in Resolven, where the largest mine in 1910 (the Rheola Colliery) employed 338 men, but the smallest (Tyra Levels) only 46, and in Glynneath, five miles up the valley, where the Pwllfaron Colliery employed 572, and the Rock Colliery 167. Unlike some of the mining valleys of the central coalfield, where ribboned housing development had led to one mining township blending into the next, the divisions marked more by custom than by urban geography, the flat-bottomed Vale of Neath retained its fields and farms, and its settlements of Resolven, Glynneath, Cwmgwrach, Blaengwrach, Pontneddfechan, Pontwalby and Aberpergwm their individuality. Whilst the Rhondda Valleys were home to over 50,000 coal miners, and the Taff to over 30,000, under 9,000 were to be found in the Vale of Neath. In contrast with the central coalfield, the anthracite area retained a semi-rural character, manifested in the customs and preferences of the population. As miners' agent John James put it:

Mae Colier y Glo Carreg yn ddyn sydd â mandrel yn yr un llaw a pâl yn y llaw arall, yn gorfforol ac ysbrydol.

(The anthracite collier has a pick in one hand and a garden spade in the other, both literally and metaphorically.)
(Ioan Matthews, 'The World of the Anthracite Miner', LLAFUR, 6, No. 1, 1992)

Stranger to neither pick nor spade, Bert Coombes found lodgings initially, and began work in a local mine as a collier's helper. Although, at first, he found the work arduous, he rapidly became acclimatized to it. Coombes's strength and resilience, attributed by him to his rural upbringing, was henceforth called upon continually over a working life of more than forty years underground. The fact that he was an Englishman in Wales, indeed in an area of Wales where the Welsh language remained strong, seems not to have troubled him. He was far from alone in this, being part of a wave of recent in-migrants. Although the 1911 Census recorded that 38 per cent of the population of the county of Glamorgan spoke Welsh (and the percentage in Resolven would have been considerably higher), the Census also recorded over 130,000 English-born in the county, representing virtually half of all those born outside its boundaries. A sixth of these in-migrants were from the West Midland counties, including Herefordshire and Staffordshire. The shared dangers of the workplace, and the need for solidarity in the face of management, rendered any ethnic divisions if not meaningless, then certainly surmountable.

In Coombes's case, the centrality of trade unionism to the south Wales miners had unenvisaged side-effects, which could only strengthen his integration within Resolven society. Calling at the house of the secretary of the local lodge of the South Wales Miners' Federation, *a great comradeship of craft*, which at that time embraced two-thirds of the mining workforce in the coalfield, Coombes met his daughter. Mary Rogers, a *dark-haired and vivacious young lady*, was of a similar age, and before long they were courting. The Rogers family was native to the town, although Mary's grandfather was of *North Welsh farming stock*. It was a Welsh-speaking family, and despite the fact that in Mary's case *there was nothing lacking in the speed and fluency of her English*, Coombes found it advantageous to learn sufficient Welsh to be able to carry on a conversation. In September 1913 they were married at St Mary's Church, Resolven, honeymooning *amongst the loaded apple orchards of Herefordshire*, and beginning a union that was to last more than fifty-six years.

There is little, in Coombes's writings, to suggest that his marriage was anything but happy. In his early, unpublished novel, 'Castell Vale' (*c*.1935), the central character Glyn Owens, who bears a strong resemblance to Coombes, is trapped in an unsatisfactory marriage with *a wife that sneers and nags at me all the time*. Jane Owens is of *dirty face, untidy hair and slovenly dress*: her death releases Glyn to marry the nurse Myfanwy Darrell, with whom he has much more in common, including a love of music. Yet here, as occasionally elsewhere, the demands of a fictional plot may have cut through Coombes's usual auto-biographical tendencies. Certainly there is no other hint of any domestic dissatisfaction in his written output. Coombes was, paradoxically given that the minutiae of his own life provided the bulk of his literary inspiration, a private, even reserved man, who found it difficult to show much outward love (*I am not easily made emotional*, he later wrote). Mary *was from a good home, and quite a worker*, she was a keen gardener, *intensely fond of flowers and animals*, and *was one of the kindest and most honest women the valleys have ever produced*, he wrote at different times. Throughout their long married life the Coombeses worked together as an effective team, nursing each other through illnesses and injuries, and planning for a future that would bring fulfilment and satisfaction to them both.

They became parents at a young age, as daughter Rose was born in 1914. For the first six years of their married life they shared rooms in a terraced house, having the use of the front room downstairs and the back room upstairs, and waiting for the kitchen to become clear to cook meals:

We had to go through the rooms of the other people for anything we wanted, even to go to the lavatories. These were the only relief to the grey stones of the streets; they were of red brick, built at the farthest end of the garden, and were placed in a high position for everyone to admire.

(THESE POOR HANDS)

When war came in August 1914, Coombes was visiting his sick mother in Herefordshire. He was so impressed by the argument that it was a 'just war', and by the *swagger* of his cousin who had joined the Military Police, that he attempted to enlist in the Hussars, only to be rejected on grounds of poor eyesight. *It was only after I came away from that office that I remembered that I, too, had a wife and child*, he observed sheepishly.

By now a hewer at the coal-face in his own right, Coombes was, from his twenty-first birthday onwards, tempted into operating a coal-cutting machine, a skill that provided him with more regular work than most in the years ahead, but which also posed its own threat to his health and even his life. Coombes appreciated the need for mechanization, but did not relish the noise, dust and increased danger that accompanied machinery. *When I think back on those days I feel we must not have known what fear was*, he wrote in THESE POOR HANDS. In 1915 he attempted to enlist in the Army a second time, only to be rejected on the grounds that he was an 'indispensable worker'.

At the end of the Great War, Coombes and his family moved from their shared rooms into 10 New Inn Place, Resolven. This was a terraced house next to a public house of that name, in the same street where Mary Coombes had been born:

It was a small house – white-washed – with two small rooms down and two up. No pantry or scullery. The front door opened towards the main road, and the other door in that room opened direct into the kitchen. There was no passage, so that if the front door was opened at the same time as the back one, we were lucky if we did not have to buy a fresh lot of dishes to replace those blown off the dresser. Having no back entrance, the returning collier, and the load of coal when it came, had to be taken through that front room, of which my wife was so proud. The floor was below the level of the street, and water ran down against the front door. At the back it was too low for any drains to act, so we had to carry all the rain-water, while in the winter we had to have a plank over the water so that we could get from

day is one spent watching the sea between the overs at St Helens (NEATH GUARDIAN, 6 April 1956).

At the end of the 1921 stoppage Coombes eventually managed to find work once more, albeit for a while at a more distant pit. In 1924 his son Peter was born, the Coombeses' second and last child. They desired more, but the cost was punitive: the 1926 strike and lock-out arrived before the debts incurred during 1921 could be redeemed, and *it took us all our time to feed and clothe* [Rose and Peter]*; there was never anything to spare* (THE LIFE WE WANT). Amidst the dramatic conflict of 1926, Coombes took the opportunity of the seven-month stoppage to develop additional skills and interests. When the St John Ambulance Association began giving free lectures in Resolven, he attended out of idleness as much as anything, but rapidly became an enthusiast for first aid and medical work, and a leading member of the local group:

Week after week we gave the only coppers we had to rent a room and buy bandages. We studied the text-book until we knew it by heart. We went under a tree on the mountain-side and bandaged each other up. We were grateful to anyone who showed us where their bones had been fractured and set; and we walked miles in each direction to attend lectures.

We borrowed bicycles and cycled more than ten miles to an important Ambulance Competition. Although we had no uniform and had to borrow equipment, we won the first prize with a margin, and out of that five pounds we bought our first stretcher, splints, and blankets. In the autumn I had an idea for funds which resulted in faking a car smash on the side of the road – with stretchers and bandaged patients – and we collected off the cars that were stopped to see what had happened.

(THESE POOR HANDS)

14

Coombes remained an active member of the St John Ambulance Association for many years, serving as sergeant and secretary of the Resolven Branch from 1932, and being awarded the Priory's Vellum Vote of Thanks for his efforts in 1972. He also trained as part of the Military Hospital Reserve, a duty which involved regular trips to Aldershot to work with the Royal Army Medical Corps. His first-aid training was, in due course, to lead him to become an underground ambulance man, a job that he combined with that of colliery repairer once he had ceased working as a machine operator.

Coombes acquired another interest during 1926: a love of music, and particularly of the violin. He began taking lessons from a local doctor, and the local chemist, who was an amateur violin-maker, made him his own instrument in 1927. Coombes helped to form the Resolven Orchestra, and also played with a quartet. His enthusiasm inspired him to save his pocket money for a whole winter so as to be able to afford a week's ticket when the National Eisteddfod visited Neath in 1934:

I do not ever expect to have more pleasure in one week. One of the national papers stated that our area was remarkably prosperous, so our colliery obliged by closing all that August week. I did not mind. I made a parcel of food and tramped the seven miles every morning. The events of each day and the glamour of the evening concerts sent me along that homeward walk happy each night.

(THESE POOR HANDS)

Only when his violin was stolen at the end of the 1930s did Coombes give up actually performing, although he retained a keen interest in music until the end of his life. In addition to these activities Coombes acted as secretary or impromptu letter-writer for a number of local societies. Always a faithful member of the South Wales Miners' Federation, he became increasingly involved in various lodge committees (including those for canteens and compensation), at the Empire Colliery, Cwmgwrach, where he obtained regular employment from the late 1920s onwards. To write of Coombes, as did David Smith ('Underground Man: The Work of B. L. Coombes, "Miner Writer"', THE ANGLO-WELSH REVIEW, 24, No. 53, Winter 1974), *that his connection with the rooted community culture* [was] *tenuous*, seems unjustifiable once the full range of his activities and involvements are appreciated. Certainly Coombes was a distinctive individual, with characteristics and enthusiasms that set him apart from many others of his occupation and class, but he was not a loner. Indeed, if one frees oneself of the need to see *the rooted community culture* simply in terms of chapels, politics and trade unionism then Coombes appears widely involved in developing many aspects of that culture through his own efforts. He was, as he admitted himself, a 'doer':

My trouble is that I become interested in almost everything I see. Then I want to go deeply into the subject, whatever it is, and am determined to do it well. Then I will not easily abandon an old interest, an old tool, or an old friend.

('Home on the Hill')

These qualities of energy, determination and dedication continued to characterize B. L. Coombes as, in the course of the 1930s, he forged a new identity for himself as a 'miner-writer'.

II

In the early 1930s, the life of B. L. Coombes – miner, ambulance man and violinist – took on a new dimension: *I started my trespass into the vast world of literature* ('I Stayed a Miner', 1957). It is not known precisely when Coombes decided to become a writer, as neither THESE POOR HANDS nor 'Home on the Hill' date this crucial event, but it seems likely that he had started by his fortieth birthday in 1933.

Coombes has left more extensive testimony as to why he decided, relatively late in life, to *start along a road, strange and alien to my surroundings* (NEATH GUARDIAN, 27 September 1963). In 'Home on the Hill' he recorded that he was inspired to write after he witnessed the death of two workmates underground. The three had been summoned by a colliery official to repair a large roof fall which had blocked the movement of coal trams. Initially, they had been unwilling to carry out the work, because the roof still looked unstable, but eventually they acquiesced: *we had to go and work in what we saw was danger because work was scarce and we had dependants.* Shortly after, both of Coombes's mates were killed instantly when a huge stone suddenly descended on them without warning from a height of eighteen feet. This was the *first time death had crashed down against my elbow.*

Coombes was the only witness to the accident, and realized that if he testified at the subsequent inquest that he and the victims had only attempted to clear the fall under protest, because the workplace appeared too dangerous, the insurance companies might seize on this as an excuse for denying compensation to the victims' dependants. Coombes's appropriately muted evidence instead led to the recording of verdicts of accidental death. At the inquest he was appalled at the ignorance he heard expressed: *I realised that neither coroner, solicitors, or hardly any one present had the least idea of what happens underground.* This episode featured in THESE POOR HANDS and in other documentary writings by Coombes, but was most memorably fictionalized in one of his best short stories, 'Twenty Tons of Coal' (NEW WRITING, 3, Christmas 1939).

It was not only the dangers of underground mining that angered Coombes; it was also the lack of appreciation of these conditions in society at large. In the NEATH GUARDIAN (27 September 1963), Coombes recalled:

At several inquests I realised how the outsiders failed to realise the hidden problems of the miners and when looking at the clean pants and shirt on the fireguard in one Aberdare house placed ready for the miner we had brought home dead, I knew somehow that the world must be better informed.

Experiences such as these were as influential for the future trajectory of Coombes's life as they were bitter at the time, as he explained in 'Home on the Hill':

Inside me somewhere was the determination that I must do something to let the world know more about our way of life. I pondered long over it, lonely in my idea, but I never forsook the intention. Months later I started to write.

Coombes decided that although he had acted as secretary for all sorts of committees and written letters for many people, he was now *going to write with a purpose. I'll try to tell the world what really happens underground and in our villages as a miner sees it* ('I Stayed a Miner').

This burning desire to tell his truth, about the lives of miners and their families, and to correct inaccuracies in public perception, was to remain the defining characteristic of Coombes's output as a writer. However, Coombes's rationale was not to provide overt, uncompromising propaganda; that, he believed, was being supplied in plenty, but was usually *so blatant that it defeats its aim.* What Coombes felt was needed was

the stories that came direct from the miners themselves. Books by working miners would increase people's knowledge and such books would endure after the speeches were forgotten.

Coombes was annoyed that trade union officials did not make miners' problems known to the wider society, but instead took the attitude that *if the outside world wants to know about miners, then the world must come to their doorstep to be informed* (NEATH GUARDIAN, 31 March 1944). Yet it was not only the world outside the coalfields that Coombes wanted to make better informed through his writing. It had often surprised him how

men can live their lives in a mining area, in many cases gaining their living almost directly from the work of miners, yet remain absolutely ignorant of the conditions of work and methods of payment in the mine.

(NEATH GUARDIAN, 13 July 1945)

Wanting to be a writer was one thing; becoming one was another, though *as usual I had considered the advantages and difficulties.* It is possible that at the outset Coombes believed he had some talent for writing: *I had read deeply for many years, had some knowledge of the use of words.* In any case, as in so much of his life, he was determined *to have a try.* He believed that writing was a craft that had to be learned, as he would later emphasize in the NEATH GUARDIAN (13 July 1945): *It is a job for an individualist who studies his craft.* Amongst those whose writing he admired were traditional favourites including Charles Dickens, the Brontës, Sir Walter Scott and James Fenimore Cooper, but Coombes drew more modern, and more political, inspiration from writers such as Robert Tressell, Lewis Grassic Gibbon, John Steinbeck, Joseph Conrad and Bret Harte.

If Coombes was to achieve his aim of becoming a writer, then there were almost insurmountable obstacles to overcome. Any assessment of Coombes's achievement as a writer must acknowledge the difficult conditions in which his writings were produced, not just in the early days, but throughout his remaining life, and the immense commitment that both he and his wife Mary gave to his new pursuit. Having left school at twelve, his education was only rudimentary, and there were severe time constraints imposed by the demands of an exhausting job, family life and union and social commitments. A further problem was that he lacked a physical space conducive to writing. In 'A Miner's Record – I' (NEW WRITING AND DAYLIGHT, Summer 1942) Coombes recalled some of the unpropitious conditions he had to face at the beginning:

I bought some pencils and three copy-books. Those, with

abounding enthusiasm and a little knowledge, were my only assets for this new venture. Against me was almost everything – heavy, exhausting toil every night in the pit, lack of room, for my writing had to be done on the kitchen table; annoyance of my wife and her friends at my appeals for quiet, and the opposition of the local brass band which practised every night in the week, except one, at the public house next door. Outside our front door children screamed and played, beer barrels were unloaded, buses and cars screeched, and when night came the bandsmen tried to blast their tunes through the wall into our room. Under those conditions I tried to sleep by day or scribble.

By 1935 the pencils and copy-books had been replaced by a *wired together typewriter* which Coombes purchased for £2. Possibly the need for *a place of retreat* in which to write was a major reason why in 1938 the Coombes family moved from New Inn Place to Oak Lodge, a cottage separated from Resolven by the main Neath Valley road. At Oak Lodge, for the first time, Coombes had a spare room. There were also financial constraints, and to offset the cost of paper Coombes often composed works on the reverse side of pages of previously typed material. Instead of purchasing files and filing cabinets, Coombes adopted a rudimentary – but effective – filing system by pegging papers on a line across the room.

An additional deterrent was the incomprehension with which those around him greeted his new aim in life: he was *laughed at by many who insisted I was wasting my time* (NEATH GUARDIAN, 27 September 1963). Even more disheartening were the rejections and rebuffs that resulted from his early efforts: *each story I sent out I thought was a masterpiece, but they came back.* Yet he *kept on* and *the copy-books were filled one after the other. I studied how to get effects, carried a little notebook to record unusual sayings and mentally described every phase of pit life to myself even when I was doing my usual job.*

('I Stayed a Miner')

By being content to learn and remember one little point or trick for each day . . . the total of that learning soon mounted. Aware of the mammoth task ahead of him, Coombes knew that he could not *achieve a worthwhile ambition and at the same time enjoy all other pleasures. Something must be paid as a sacrifice in return.* Never a great drinker, Coombes largely avoided pubs. Although he had a great admiration for Charlie Chaplin, he preferred long walks in the hills to visits to the cinema. Holidays, beyond trips to Porthcawl, were as rare as days of rest. It was perhaps then fortunate for him that *reading or writing, those activities which give the majority of people headaches, seemed to charm my pains away* ('A Miner's Record – I').

In the early years Coombes struggled with his style, trying to develop one he *could wear like a skin.* The model he followed was that of THE BIBLE, where there was *no waste of wording, direct and clear.* His own justification for his constant striving for *directness and simplicity in the written and the spoken word* reveals an umbilical link between style and purpose: *I feel that simplicity is an essential to good writing; especially if a writer hopes to be read by the mass of the people* ('A Miner's Record – I'). He was also convinced of the need for humour, and in his essay 'Below the Tower' (FOLIOS OF NEW WRITING, 3, Spring 1941) regretted that often in the case of working-class writers *it seems the struggle has made them grim and that their characters have either a perpetual snarl or a whine. This is not true to life for even in the hardest conditions and heaviest work there is always humour flashing out. We have found things to laugh over when shut in - for ever it seemed - by a huge fall.*

Although Coombes claimed in the NEATH GUARDIAN (13 July 1945) that he *soon realised I had to rely on my own efforts,* and that in *the writing business you must prove yourself, alone and unaided before your worth is accepted,* he was not entirely without assistance and advice in the first years of his writing. He joined local classes run by the National Council of Labour Colleges (NCLC), taking courses in intermediate English and chairmanship, and he became one of the organization's postal students. Later he paid tribute to the *much-appreciated assistance in the form of searching criticism and constructive advice* he received from his tutors and acknowledged that *I owe these classes a debt I shall not forget* (NEATH GUARDIAN, 30 June 1944). He also praised the NCLC in an early article, 'Can We Have Educated Slaves?', which appeared in the 'Battle of Ideas' column in REYNOLDS NEWS in August 1937. NCLC classes, he wrote, were a necessary antidote to the *old exploiting system* and the *dope* learned at school because independent education *forced the student to think out his own problems.*

By 1934, Coombes, writing under the pseudonym 'Becomb', had joined the 'British Scribbler' writing circle which had been initiated by two Oxford dons in 1900. Under the scheme, aspirant writers circulated stories and plays for mutual and constructive criticism and, initially, Coombes may have aimed to become a creative writer. For his raw material he drew largely on episodes he had experienced himself, from the outset establishing the strongly autobiographical dimension that would characterize most of his writing.

In about 1934 or 1935, Coombes also began what was the first of many attempts at writing a novel, though his ambition to be a novelist, which he expressed on a number of occasions, would never be fulfilled. 'Castell Vale' was probably completed during the mid-1930s, but only about half of it survives in manuscript, and it is not known if it was sent to a publisher. The novel is set in 'Rescwm', a mining community located in 'Castell Vale', and it traces the developing romance of miner and violinist Glyn Owens and Myfanwy Darrell. In its barest outline the plot seems improbable and contrived, but 'Castell Vale' does contain some memorable passages which bring to life the social and cultural activities of mining communities. It is also an early exploration of themes other than mining which would feature in Coombes's writing, including the importance of music, and the attachment he had to the land.

As well as short stories, plays and novels, in his early years Coombes also engaged in documentary and political writing, with some degree of success and recognition. In 1935 his first published article, 'Distressed', a bitter critique of the National Government's Distressed Areas Policy, appeared in the political magazine WELSH LABOUR OUTLOOK (1, No. 2, January 1935). He also began to send entries to literary competitions, submitting a one-act play 'Closed' to the 1935 National Eisteddfod at Caernarfon. In 1936 he was one of three prize-winners in an essay competition, 'What Life Means to Me', run by LEFT REVIEW (December 1936).

In the same vein as his attack on the government in 'Distressed' and 'Can We Have Educated Slaves?', 'What Life Means to Me' is a brief but deeply political essay, showing, in embryo, Coombes's bitterness at the waste of human life and potential in the South Wales Coalfield during the inter-war years. It also sets out for the first time the ideas and views that would be developed in his later and more extensive writings. Life, Coombes writes,

means a continual hurrying to the call of the hooter and going underground away from the sun, the fresh air, the song of the birds and the sight of the trees. It means long days of straining effort while the sweat runs into my eyes, stones cut pieces from my body and my lungs fill with dust.

Coombes goes on to fear for the future of the children of mining families (*their prospects do not seem very good under the present system*), but also insists that existing conditions must improve (*that system will – it must – be changed before their day of trial*) and to achieve that end he vows he will devote *every spare breath, every thought . . . Not for my own benefit, but the benefit of the majority of those who are coming after us.* Such anger and combativeness are complemented by things which make his life bearable: walking, discussing, attending lodge meetings, sitting in the library *to travel in company with Jack London* and *hate in sympathy with Upton Sinclair, Sinclair Lewis and Dos Passos* (and avoid *the froth of the 'popular novelists' and the fairy tales of the* DAILY EXPRESS), and finally receiving the LEFT BOOK CLUB choice and the LEFT REVIEW every month. During the following three years he would see his own work in both.

III

The latter part of 1936 marks a significant turning-point in B. L. Coombes's writing career, and one which would have great bearing on his subsequent development. Towards the end of that year his short story 'The Flame' was accepted by John Lehmann, the poet, and also publisher and editor of NEW WRITING (NEW WRITING, 3, Spring 1937). 'The Flame' brought Coombes to the attention of a much wider audience, and in Lehmann it earned Coombes a friend and mentor whose influence became so crucial that it was to him that Coombes dedicated THESE POOR HANDS.

Coombes was just the type of writer that Lehmann was eager to discover and promote: working-class writers who had no educational advantages and *when they wrote of mines, seamen, factory workers or East End tailors, were writing from the inside, out of their own experiences* (THE WHISPERING GALLERY, 1955). In NEW WRITING Lehmann sought to break down social and creative barriers, and to obtain a cross-fertilization of talents between working-class writers on the one hand, and educated, middle-class authors and poets (such as Christopher Isherwood, Stephen Spender, W. H. Auden and George Orwell) on the other. Lehmann later testified to the impact Coombes's work had upon him:

What struck me at once about 'The Flame' . . . was the simplicity and unforced, quiet movement of the writing with its occasional small touches that revealed the natural way of talking of the West of England. This rare quality – for men who have no formal education beyond elementary school too often use the jargon of newspapers and the lurid style of cheap novelettes when they try to write – was allied, as story after story showed, with a capacity to make you feel exactly what it was like to be alone in a mine.

As with nearly all of Coombes's short stories, 'The Flame' fictionalizes an actual experience, later described in 'Home on the Hill':

At one time I worked in a seam no more than eighteen inches high . . . One day a pocket of gas caught as I was charging a hole with dynamite. So low was the roof that I could not get up to run. I could have got away no quicker than a slow swimmer so I lay tight to the ground and hoped. The flash of gas flickered past the detonator, and the dynamite, but for some marvellous reason no explosion happened.

It is a measure of Coombes's talent and developing skills as an imaginative writer that this terrifying episode was transformed into a taut, compressed masterpiece. It opens with Jack Davies, a collier, in his workplace underground, preparing a fuse in order to blast down the coal. The reader is taken through each stage of the process in meticulous detail, emphasizing Jack's skill and experience (he works *with a swiftness that showed how used he was to the semi-darkness*) and the routine yet dangerous nature of the work.

He did not trouble to move his lamp but reached into the darkness to grab the three cartridges of dynamite from the canister. He loosened the paper at the end of one and jabbed the knife-blade in to make a hole. He reached a small tin from a ledge and took from it a copper object – a bullet-shaped detonator so delicately tempered that the least jar would explode it – and blew sharply into the open end. At his third blow the dull whistle that resulted assured Jack that all the sawdust had been cleared out so he pushed one end of the fuse into the small circle and tightened the 'cap' by biting the end with his teeth – as if the detonator held chocolate instead of fulminate of mercury.

Jack is alone, seemingly comfortable in his solitude:

He had no company, so he spoke his thoughts aloud – confident that even though the words echoed very loudly through the hollow workings there was no one who would be near enough to hear his complaint.

His wry sense of humour is also evident, as when he accidentally walks into a tram:

That's another bit outer me shin . . . It 'ud be a lot better if they wus to pay us for the bumps we get instead of the coal as we fills.

But there is no denying the sheer physical discomfort of his working conditions (the seam is *not more than twenty inches thick – and it was so solid that every scrap must be blasted*), in which even the simplest tasks demand strenuous effort:

With his stomach pressed against the bottom and his back tight against the top Jack started to force his body the six yards to the shot-hole. The downhill slope of the ground helped him to get there; but the same slope would be a severe handicap when he wanted to return. As he went down, so he must get back. It was impossible to turn around and he would not be able to rush backward but would have to wriggle back slowly, feeling with his feet and guessing his direction, until the pressure on his back would ease and he could step to his feet.

Jack successfully sets off one charge, although because the air is so thin, the smoke does not clear, but thickens and remains solid *like a blue wall*. The smoke makes it even more difficult to see, and causes Jack to cough and sneeze (*it was acrid and burning in his throat and chest*). He prepares a second charge and, *at full length*, proceeds to bore another hole in that confined space. Because of the smoke, however, the work is even harder:

The second ramming was torture, for in that small space the stench and smoke of the powder was overpowering and his lungs were too cramped to clear themselves. The water ran from his eyes so that he could scarcely see what he did.

He pushes the dynamite and the detonator into the hole until only the fuse shows outside it. However, he cannot find the clay he has prepared to tamp the hole. As he searches for it he discovers something else:

He had placed his lamp as far as possible from the powder charge and the hole and when he managed to turn his head enough to see the lamp-flame he saw another flame that turned his annoyance to chill fear.

It was a thin flame - dancing and blue as the one seen on a coal fire – and with gay little hops it was flitting swiftly towards the end of the fuse – the hole – the delicate cap – and the dynamite.

In an instant Jack guesses that an unexpected presence of gas had touched the naked flame of his carbide lamp and was now running down the coal edge to the shot-hole. This seemingly innocent and playful flame (which when it ignited the fuse *began to flash and sparkle like a child's firework*) is deadly and

Jack tries to grab it with both hands, but his cramped position prevents him. Nor, he quickly realizes, is he able to escape back to safety along the low passage. He is trapped and can only watch the flame advance. The suspense heightens as each stage of the flame's progress towards the hole is charted until

the blue flame swirled, made what sounded like a faint 'plop'; then disappeared down the hole towards the powder; and in that instant Jack gave up his hopes of life and pushed his face into the small coal while he shielded his head with his hands.

In that moment as Jack waits for the blast, thoughts rush through his mind. He entertains the *vague hope* that his body will not be too disfigured, even though the dynamite is less than two yards from his face. He wonders who will be the first to discover his body, how long before they would find it, and how his wife Nancy and his mother would take the news. He waits and waits:

Then he thought – this will be the last second – no – this one – no, this one. Then he thought – it's bound to happen before I count to five and he counted them slowly as if he did not want to be proved wrong.

Then he realised that a minute – no, two minutes must have passed and he was still alive.

Jack is incredulous that he might escape an otherwise inevitable death, his disbelief forcing him to stay crouched in his position until *the complete silence around him convinced him that something unexpected had saved him.* He starts to move back out of what so easily could have been his tomb, still keeping his face covered. When he is level with the shot-hole *he uncovered one eye and peeped along it. He saw no sign of flame. Almost hysterical with relief,* he realizes that either the flame has jumped over the dynamite cap or – a shaking irony – the lack of air that had made Jack's breathing difficult has also extinguished his potential killer. But the story does not end on a note of relief or celebration. The normality of facing extraordinary dangers every ordinary day is reasserted, and work – and making a living – has to carry on.

'The Flame' brought Coombes letters of appreciation and requests for more of his work from editors in the United States, among them Simon Schuster and Borzoi Books (the American publishers of NEW WRITING), who both expressed interest in whether Coombes was writing a novel. Coombes himself recalled that this triumph gave greater momentum to his writing: *I suppose the knowledge of success makes you more energetic* ('I Stayed a Miner'). The appearance in 1938 of two other stories which he had written during 1937, 'Better Off' and 'Machine Man' (NEW WRITING, 5, Spring 1938), further enhanced his growing reputation as a writer. Like 'The Flame', both these stories had a firm basis in Coombes's actual experiences, and both reaffirm the effectiveness of Coombes's graphic, understated narrative, his vivid depiction and his ability to involve the reader intimately in the story's development.

In 'Better Off' a miner receives a letter informing him that his widowed mother has died. Towards the end of her life, as her illness worsened, she had been admitted to the infirmary at the local workhouse in her native, rural area, having refused to move to live with her son and his family in the mining village to which he had migrated. The story portrays the miner's feelings of loss, sadness and guilt at the news, and his growing anger at the hard life his mother had had to endure and at the manner in which he had been told of her death. She had not merited a telegram

or even a letter of regret written on decent notepaper . . . Yet she had worked hard all her life, had tried to be decent, and had never known the least luxury.

The story has subtle variations in tempo as, still staring at the letter, the miner both works out the arrangements he must make for the funeral and contemplates his mother's life. In this way Coombes effectively conveys how the mind, on hearing unexpected news of the death of a loved one, ricochets from one thought to the next, trying to get to grips with necessary practicalities yet at the same time wanting to dwell on memories and to grieve. The miner wonders whether his mother will now have the contentment and peace she was denied on earth:

she had not had much of the good things of this life, so surely she would qualify for the greater happiness that was promised in Heaven.

His lengthy brooding is eventually only broken by his thirteen-year-old son's intervention, speaking *loudly and definitely, as one would who is sure they are correct: 'Don't you worry, dad. She's a lot better off.'*

Whereas 'Better Off' bleakly questions whether ordinary working people will ever be rewarded for their hard work and suffering, 'Machine Man', which Lehmann accepted in January 1938, returns to the dangers faced by miners every day of their working lives underground. The main character is Don Hughes, the driver of a coal-cutting machine. As in 'The Flame', a seemingly innocuous incident escalates into a potentially fatal situation when Don, like Jack Davies, is alone and out of reach of help, and he only escapes a gruesome death by pure chance. Coombes again relies on an almost dispassionate telling of the facts of the story to convey a horrific series of events.

Needing to erect timbers at the face, yet unwilling to switch off the machine as this would halt production and incur the wrath of the management, Don lies on top of the moving coal-cutter in order to ease his task. However, as the cutter approaches a much narrower part of the seam where there is a gap of only four inches between its top and the roof, Don suddenly realizes he cannot get off as the buttonhole of his waistcoat is caught on a nut. He tries, with mounting desperation, to scream for help, to wriggle off or to reach the cutter's control switch, but to no avail. As the machine moves relentlessly on, it seems inevitable that Don will be crushed. Yet, making one last attempt to jerk forward, Don knocks his sledge-hammer into the path of the cutter's picks. The hammer's head is too hard for the picks and the machine blows a fuse and stops.

One of the impressive features of 'Machine Man' is the way in which Coombes succeeds in detailing every action which first threatens to kill Don, then allows him to live. By slowing down what would, in reality, have taken only a matter of seconds, Coombes increases the tension and speeds up the momentum of the narration. The story ends with a matter-of-fact acceptance, almost chilling in the light of what has happened:

He was free and had repaired the switch by the time Fred returned.

'Hallo,' Fred was surprised, 'she's stopped. What's up?'

'Nearly got squeezed,' Don was laconic, 'just had me, she did.'

'Huh.' Close escapes were part of their job, and Fred was used to them. 'And I've been crawling all over the blasted pit a'looking for timber. Pretty fed-up I am.'

'And the sledge is broke,' Don added.

'Broke! By Gosh!' Fred was surprised, 'then we're in a proper hole. S'pose as we'll have to pinch one off the colliers.'

During 1937 and 1938, as he grew in confidence and his literary output increased, Coombes gained other forms of recognition. He continued to enter various literary competitions, winning a DAILY HERALD prize for an essay (on the life of a colliery ambulance man) in April 1937, and a silver medal for an original story at the Borough of Leyton Eisteddfod in 1938. He was also invited to review books for LIFE AND LETTERS TO-DAY and the DAILY WORKER. Though the actual reviews were often little more than notices, they signalled a recognition of his existence as a writer and commentator. Coombes also became a prodigious correspondent and a dedicated self-publicist, writing letters to newspapers and fellow writers all over Britain. If one considers that during 1937 he was also writing THESE POOR HANDS, Coombes's work rate at this time was astonishing.

The fame of both THESE POOR HANDS and Coombes's documentary writing on mining and mining communities can obscure the fact that he first achieved recognition as a short-story writer. In 1939 he published his best-known story, 'Twenty Tons of Coal'. As noted earlier, the raw material for this had been the death of two workmates alongside him underground (although only one features in the short story). It was an experience of which he felt compelled, cathartically, to write:

still hanging in my memory like a bad dream was the thought of that fatal accident and the deaths of Danny and Phil. Now, more competent, I had to write it, and the words went down red hot on the pages.

('I Stayed a Miner')

'Twenty Tons of Coal' falls into three unequal parts. It opens with the anonymous narrator, who has survived the accident that killed his mate Griff, exploring the intensity of the shock and dread from which he is suffering:

my inside trembles now as it did when this thing occurred . . . I have been afraid to close my eyes because of the memory that darkness brings.

He is waiting to attend the inquest, terrified by *every sudden word or slam of the door,* dreading the darkness *which had held my mate but allowed me to escape.* To prepare himself for the forthcoming ordeal he tries *to recall what happened and whisper it to myself in such a way that I shall be question-proof when the time comes.*

The bulk of the story consists of a step-by-step narrative of the hours before, during and immediately after the accident. Griff, whom the reader knows will shortly be killed, is introduced *sitting near the lamp-room*, finishing his pipe of tobacco before descending the pit. He is fifty years old, *well built but quite inoffensive*, a moderate drinker and an enthusiast for rugby football. Griff and the narrator, both repairers, are dispatched to clear a fall of rock, but the roof remains unstable:

Stones that have been walled on the sides are crumbling from the pressure and there sounds a continual crack-crack as timber breaks or stones rip apart. As we stand by, a thick post starts to split down the middle and the splitting goes on while we watch, as if an invisible giant was tearing it in half. Alongside us another post that is quite two foot in diameter snaps in the middle and pieces of the bark fly into our faces.

Clearing the fall is thirsty work: when Griff drinks water it *gurgled down his throat as it would have down a drain*. After some hours they stop for food, shortly after which they are called to another fall, which is blocking a journey of coal trams. This time the state of the roof is even more precarious. The narrator wants to put up timber to secure it, but the fireman insists that they clear the rock as quickly as possible, or else lose their jobs. Faced with this ultimatum they press on, *breaking the big stones and rolling them back one on top of another*:

We had cleared about half of the fall and I had finished breaking a large stone when Griff asked me for the sledge-hammer. Our elbows touched when I handed it to him. As he hit with the sledge I lifted a stone on to my knees but it slid down and dropped a couple of feet from the rail. I moved a short pace after it, bent, then began to lift it again. When I was almost straightened up I felt air rushing past my face; something hit me a terrible blow on the back. I heard a sound that seemed to start as a sob but ended in a groan that was checked abruptly. The blow on the back hit me forward. I felt to be flung along the roadway whilst my face ploughed through the small coal on the floor of the heading. I am sure that fire flashed from my eyes, yet I felt at the same time to be ice-cold all over. My legs were dead weights hanging behind me. When I breathed I swallowed the small coal that was inside my mouth. My nose was blocked with dust, so were my eyes. I felt about with my hands before realizing that my face was against the floor and pushing down my arms to lift myself. I whimpered with relief when I found I could use my legs and so my back was not broken.

At least twenty tons of rock had fallen. Eventually, with many men working together to try and rescue the situation, the largest stone is lifted, and *very carefully they drew out what had been Griff.* He

seems to be no more than half his usual size. Someone takes his watch from the waistcoat hanging on the side. They hold the shining back against what they believe is his mouth.

The men carry Griff's body on a stretcher back to his home, to wash him in his kitchen. *Neighbours have been busy . . . A large fire is burning, the tub is in, water is steaming on the hob,* and from upstairs can be heard *a sound of sobbing* from Griff's wife. As for his five children, their voices *are soft and subdued, as if they had only partly wakened and had not yet realized the disaster this dawn had brought to them.* With the interests of Griff's family at heart, the story ends with the narrator explaining that he must lie about the circumstances of the accident in order for them to be sure of receiving compensation:

at four o'clock I will be at the inquest, shall kiss the Bible, and speak 'The whole truth and nothing but the truth' – perhaps. Would you?

'Twenty Tons of Coal' is a much longer work than 'The Flame' and 'Machine Man', and was immediately recognized as a major achievement; Lehmann considering it *outstanding*. Its power stems from the tense expectation implicit in the narrative from the very outset; from the uncompromising depiction of the accident and its impact upon a human body that only a page or so before was drinking, sweating and joking; and from the extent of the mental damage that evidently has been wreaked upon the narrator himself. It is a moral tale: Griff and his family have been victimized by nature, the mine management, the compensation system and the insecurity that stalks the lives of the working class. These injustices seep from the story, much as Coombes described the weight of the roof squeezing out the turpentine from the wooden posts that were trying to hold it up.

The late 1930s was the high point of Coombes's career as a short-story writer. After this time he did not write many more stories, despite encouragement by Lehmann and others, and his own interest in the techniques of the craft. Two were published in wartime: 'Sabbath Night' (FOLIOS OF NEW WRITING, 2, Autumn 1940) and 'Thick Candles' (PENGUIN NEW WRITING, 1944). As one critic observed at the time, 'Sabbath Night' is more a work of social reportage than of imaginative fiction, suggesting perhaps that Coombes had failed in what often seems to have been a struggle to keep his documentary impulses in check when writing fiction. Four more stories were published after the end of the Second World War, all of them in COAL.

It can be argued that Coombes was a short-story writer of no mean talent, yet, one suspects, possessed of only a limited range. In some senses his potential as a short-story writer was never fulfilled. Perhaps he was deterred by his own experiences in writing them:

I found that the writing and revising of a short story . . . maintaining my own interest, and my reader's all the while was no small task. My enthusiasm and temper usually got a little frayed before I got half way and those things show in the writing.

('The Working-Class Writer', 1947)

Rather than dedicate his energies to this demanding genre, increasingly Coombes moved into the writing of non-fiction. He came to regard social documentary as the best means through which he might achieve his unique mission as a writer.

IV

Mr Coombes' exact descriptions, born of his own experience, will receive abundant corroboration from those who know colliery life at first hand, and ought to be welcomed and valued by those more fortunate people who have never had to grope in the guts of the earth for a living.

This sixpenny book is probably the most truthful account of a miner's life yet written. Anyway, I have not come across a better one.

(Idris Davies, LIFE AND LETTERS TO-DAY, 21, 1939)

The significance of B. L. Coombes's I AM A MINER, which appeared as the twenty-third pamphlet in the FACT series in February 1939, was quickly over-shadowed by the publication of THESE POOR HANDS just four months later. Yet, as the words of the poet, teacher and ex-miner Idris Davies suggested, Coombes's study merited critical praise as a fine example of a 'worker-autobiography' in its own right. It had been commissioned by FACT's editors in August 1938 eager, generally, to have *working-class writers who will give us Facts* and, specifically, to have a companion volume to an earlier pamphlet in the series. Philip Massey's PORTRAIT OF A MINING TOWN, a sociological account of Nantyglo and Blaina in Monmouthshire, had appeared in 1937, and it was thought that a 'self-portrait' by a working miner might provide an ideal complement to his rigor-ous, but somewhat detached study, Massey having aimed to conduct his survey *as truthfully and penetratingly as if* [he] *had been inspecting an African village.*

I AM A MINER falls into two distinct halves. The first three chapters – *To the Pithead, One Shift (1),* and *One Shift (2)* – provide a succinct account of the working day of B. L. Coombes, the 'universal' miner. Chapters 4 to 7 – *Pay Envelopes, Miners' Town, The Boys* and *Accident and Death* – stand, largely independent of each other, as documentary treatments of distinct themes in the work and life of coalfield society.

The first half of the book opens with an unenthusiastic Coombes boarding the bus that will take him to Friday's night-shift at the mine, the last of the week. He sits with his companions, who are indifferent to the three religious posters that decorate the bus. The text of each is used as a prompt for Coombes's own message. The first – *Love one another? Huh! Better send that one to the coal-owners* – receives swift dismissal, but the second – *The wages of sin are death* – generates a more expansive response:

I know there are other, and less romantic ways of getting that reward, for I have seen ample evidence of death, suffering, and semi-starvation coming to honest and hard-working men through no fault of their own.

The third dictum – *'I am the Light of the world'* – allows Coombes to express, without reservation, his belief in the importance of his work:

. . . the furtive sunlight of this day has faded over the mountains and we are on our way to produce the mineral that is so essential to replace and assist it in giving heat, light, and

41

*working power to the people of this land; to take our part in
bringing out from the darkness that black substance that has ten
thousand years of compressed sunlight in its forming and a
hundred uses when formed; and which brings such poor
rewards to its hewers but great wealth to its exploiters – COAL.*

As the bus nears the mine Coombes explains the
different jobs the work demands – repairers, colliers,
engine drivers, fitters, labourers – all *sit silently as if
they were being carried to a battle*. He draws attention
to the long hours workers spend in travel to and
from the mine, to the need for pit-head baths, and
speculates on the damage done to the lungs and
intestines by coal dust. When the bus arrives at the
colliery an ambulance is there, *not an unusual sight*,
taking an injured boy to the hospital. As the men
climb the incline to the mine they pass the afternoon
shift on the way down, and then begin the night's
work.

The journey to the coal-face is two miles in length.
Coombes describes the blackness, the heat, the
smoke and dust that hang in the air; the stench
that emanates from rotting timber, dead rats and
excreta both human and animal; the manholes cut
into the sides of the roadways which allow shelter
from passing trams; the horses and cats that live
underground; and the tools that greet them when
they arrive at the face. Coombes, with other
repairers, is engaged in clearing a fall of rock: the
work demands care, strength, endurance and alert-
ness to any sign of movement in the roof above.
Interrupted to help a rider place a tram back on the
rails, at 3 a.m. they stop for their meal, before
assisting in the placing of posts to hold up the roof.
In passing, Coombes tells of the different types of

coal with which he has worked, of the high levels of productivity, and of danger generated by coal-cutting machinery and the use of conveyors underground. Eventually it is time to leave, and emerging into the dazzling sunlight the shift checks off. As the bus takes the black-faced men back to their homes they doze in their seats.

Throughout the first half of I AM A MINER Coombes combines an individual narrative (what happens to him during one, unremarkable, shift) with documentary-style reportage of the general conditions under which mining is carried out. This is an extremely effective technique for enlisting the sympathy and interest of the reader, and it is one that he used many times in different genres. The explicit didacticism of the opening passages gives way to a more relaxed and subtle instruction: Coombes does not need to ram home his points because the simple descriptions of his working environment perform this function without prompting.

The discussion of the system by which miners are paid and the detail that is supplied of petty injustices, complete with sample weight ticket and pay docket, reinforce the general sense of embattlement that characterizes the opening chapters. *There are managements who observe the custom of the coalfield,* admits Coombes, but *others are minor – or miner – dictators,* and *there are many ways of penalizing a miner who is too insistent on his rights.*

The aftermath of pay-day in a 'miners' town' is given glorious treatment in the fifth chapter, a most sensitive, rounded and acute observation of coalfield society, and one that surely contradicts David

Smith's view that *Coombes is not a guide to the intricate life of the mining townships.*

Here we have depiction of the women, who, *by slaving all their waking hours . . . manage to defy the greyness outside and make the inside bright,* and who

are always cleaning and polishing – or hurrying along the passage to see whether that motor-car they can hear coming is the colliery ambulance or the bailiff's van.

On pay-day the carts of greengrocers and fish-and-chip merchants mingle in the streets with cockle women, tallymen and insurance collectors. Once the miners have returned home, then, after a brief delay,

there are hurried exits of housewives who have dressed themselves with care and carry a shopping bag slung over their arms and a satchel tightly held in their hand.

These, on their way to Neath, are followed by those hurrying to fill in the football pools at the Post Office. On a Saturday afternoon there is the rugby match; in the evening the pictures, and the pub. Sunday is *a day of parades*, with men out walking their dogs, cyclists and ramblers setting out for their hours of exercise, and the *more lethargic* congregating on the streets. Chapel-goers hurry past, *with an air of having forgotten the collection money*, and *the walkers sniff as eagerly at the smell of cooking meat as they had inhaled the mountain air on the outward journey*. In the afternoon the young parade past each other, *alert for mischief or adventure*, and Sunday evenings see the chapels at their fullest. Coombes comments on coal-stealing, on the dramatic societies and choirs, and on the *keenness for books* at the libraries of the miners' institute. This is a democratic, participatory culture, whose spirit surges through Coombes's prose:

There is no one who can be counted rich in this area. The rich people who control our lives live at a considerable distance from here. So anyone who is in trouble can be fairly sure of help and sympathy. Everyone is interested in the injury or illness of another and the majority of houses are open-doored to anyone who may call. When a funeral happens, all who can possibly get there attend it, for as an old collier remarked, 'We'll all want somebody to carry us to the grave if we lives long enough.' The clothes we wear are not important; it is the respect that we try to show that matters.

The final two chapters of I AM A MINER deal with those whom Coombes feels to be particularly at risk from the harsh environment of coal mining. Boys suffer from a high accident rate and low wages, and, writing of his own son, Coombes says that although he will soon want work, *the last possible avenue will be to the mines.* For some of those who do enter the industry, awaiting them might be an early death from silicosis or anthracosis, mutilation or paralysis by underground accident, or the long-term damage of neurasthenia and nystagmus. The compensation rules deter the reporting of smaller accidents, and *most of the miners are tough and have a contempt for small injuries.* Contrasting the profits and royalties made from the coal industry with the poor levels of remuneration and compensation that miners endure, Coombes ends I AM A MINER by wondering *is a working-man of any greater value than the dust? Sometimes I think he is not.*

I AM A MINER, Christine Millar believed, was an ideal book for

presentation for those members of the public for whom the word 'miner' signifies underfeeding the family to get titbits for the whippet, 'squandering high wages on horses and pools,' or loafing on the dole.

('A Spotlight on Mining', PLEBS, 31, No. 4, April 1939)

Coombes's matter-of-fact, restrained style communicated the essential humanity of coal miners alongside the stark inhumanity of their surroundings and treatment. It was a style he was to deploy to even greater effect in THESE POOR HANDS.

V

Although it was published in June 1939, Coombes completed THESE POOR HANDS: THE AUTOBIOGRAPHY OF A MINER WORKING IN SOUTH WALES in the course of 1937, sent it to the left-wing publisher Victor Gollancz that autumn, and had it accepted for publication in March 1938. Gollancz himself read the work twice in manuscript, before writing to Coombes (20 February 1939) to tell him that *your book should stir the conscience of people more than any book published for very many years.* Gollancz believed that THESE POOR HANDS could *throw a searchlight on civilisation as it is here in England* [sic] *to-day,* and his recommendation that it should be selected as 'Book of the Month' by the Left Book Club was endorsed by the political scientist Harold Laski and the poet and novelist L. A. G. Strong. This endorsement ensured that sales of THESE POOR HANDS immediately exceeded 60,000 copies: in fact, nearly 80,000 volumes were sold within the first year, at a time when few books sold more than 50,000. With over 1,200 Left Book Club local groups in existence across Britain, THESE POOR HANDS was discussed from Falkirk to Canterbury and from Weston-super-Mare to Newcastle upon Tyne, and a syllabus and notes for discussion were circulated to local Club leaders to assist them in focusing the response of the left-leaning reading public. Coombes himself received letters complimenting him on his achievement from friends and strangers across Britain and the Empire: some miners, some writers, others Welsh exiles. In due course THESE POOR HANDS was translated and published in many European languages, including Russian. It was Coombes's single most important achievement as a 'miner-writer', and one whose fame and impact he was never to surpass.

The majority of published reviews also welcomed THESE POOR HANDS. PUNCH (9 August 1939) considered it *an excellent piece of objective writing, in which humour and a gift of quick description are marked*, and the NEATH GUARDIAN (23 June 1939) thought it *a virile work crowded with interest*. The book found an enthusiastic reception on the political left. Labour MP John Strachey, writing in LEFT NEWS (June 1939), felt that Coombes had produced a work *which hardly anyone could read without great pleasure and without great emotion*, and novelist, critic and short-story writer V. S. Pritchett, writing in the NEW STATESMAN AND NATION (2 September 1939) considered THESE POOR HANDS *an honest, humane document, absorbing in its simplicity and dignity*. Some on the extreme left, such as the Communist Idris Cox in LABOUR MONTHLY (September 1939), acknowledged that *as a piece of descriptive writing on the dangers and trials of a miner's life there is nothing to beat this book*, but worried that Coombes himself did *not seem capable of drawing any political conclusions* and was *not yet convinced that our job is to change the world as well as describe it*. However, fellow Communist Arthur Horner, president of the South Wales Miners' Federation, thought that on balance

it is better to have a straightforward simple life story of a miner, for the facts revealed will speak for themselves in such a manner as to win the support of all honest people for the miners.
(DAILY WORKER, 28 June 1939)

The most consistent criticism of the reviewers of THESE POOR HANDS was that it was insufficiently autobiographical. In LIFE AND LETTERS TO-DAY (22, 1939) a fellow working-class writer, the taxi-driver Herbert Hodge, thought Coombes to be

one of the most modest men who ever attempted autobiography. He tells us hardly anything about himself – no more than the minimum of personal detail necessary to explain his reactions to the mine.

Glyn Jones lamented in THE WELSH REVIEW (2, No. 2, September 1939) that THESE POOR HANDS was too *exclusively concerned* with coal mining as an occupation, and that Coombes was *an incurable talker of shop*:

I kept on wishing he could come out from behind his coal dust oftener and tell us more about himself as a human being – about his family and his cricket, and his fiddle, and his writing of course.

In many respects such criticisms are justified: THESE POOR HANDS is not a conventional autobiography. It opens with Coombes on the verge of both manhood and departure from Herefordshire, and gives very little information about either his family or his childhood. Coombes, like many working-class autobiographers, may not have thought the details of his private life worthy of comment, or particularly relevant to his purpose in writing. Few dates are to be found throughout the rest of the book, making it difficult for the reader to pinpoint precisely the unfolding chronology of Coombes's life. Coombes excises many place-names, and names only a small cast of characters, not including his wife Mary. It is difficult to escape the conclusion that Coombes made all these decisions deliberately, simplifying the complexities of his own life in order to render his story one that could be recognized by miners the world over. The more anonymous he could make his autobiography, the more universal his message would appear.

The achievement of a sense of universality, rather than particularity, was assisted by the book's structure. Although its fourteen chapters follow one another in rough chronological order, beginning in c.1908 and including the last contemporary references of c.1934, the historical narrative does not progress in a straightforward fashion, frequently being interrupted by contemporary observation, with Coombes often mixing past and present tenses in the same paragraph. The final two chapters are expressly contemporary and immediate. Moreover, Coombes oscillates between relating his own experiences and the more general reactions of his fellow miners, be these in his colliery, his valley or even in the coalfield at large. THESE POOR HANDS becomes not so much his story, as the story of the hundreds of thousands of miners in south Wales and in Britain as a whole.

Coombes's success in conveying the sense that his single life was representative of a multiple experience rested largely on his judicious selection and description of key themes in mining life. First, he has to establish himself as an authentic witness of what he sees around him, and achieves this through a succession of detailed vignettes, such as that of his first working place:

It was known as the Deep. We were the lowest place of all, because this Deep was heading into the virgin coal to open work. Every fifty yards on each side of our heading other headings opened left and right, but they would be working across the slope, and so were running level. From these level headings the stalls were opening to work all the coal off.

There follows a precise account of how difficult the work is to a newcomer: the need to acquire certain techniques in handling a shovel, in coping with the dark, the dust, the water and the new demands on one's body. Occasionally Coombes breaks off from the historical narrative, in almost conversational style, for the benefit of his readers:

Perhaps I should explain what is meant by a lid and a post? A post is a piece of timber, either foreign or home-grown, which is set at an angle to meet the slope of the roof. It must be set solidly in a hole at the butt, but is usually measured so that a space of four or five inches is left on top. Another flattened piece of timber is then driven over the post at right angles. This shorter piece – or lid – tightens the post, and also presents a much greater length of support to the roof.

The constant battle the miners face is not just with the elements underground, but also with the colliery management, in ensuring that they get fair remuneration for work done. The latter are always out to cheat the miner – *bullies who were intent on avoiding payment for work done* says Coombes's first 'butty' John, presented as an upright, solid chap, worthy of Coombes's, and our, respect. Coombes skilfully conveys the impression that he arrived in the mines without any preconceived ideas about the nature of industrial relations in the coal industry, yet rapidly discovered the truth of this relationship through his own experience and through the testimony of his work-comrades. The mine management are, with few exceptions, presented as devious, dishonest and often ignorant, their chief ambition being to cheat the miner of the full reward for his arduous labour. Coombes explains that he himself had fallen victim to one such trick, when along with his friend Tommy Davies he had been tempted into filling more trams for higher wages (an extra pound), only to find that their rate of cutting was then used as the norm by which to set the price list, ensuring that no miner ever earned more than the minimum wage in that district thereafter. The saving grace, as far as Coombes is concerned, is that the experience radicalized him into union activism:

My regret over the result of this episode and the knowledge that it was our youth and inexperience that had allowed us to make this mistake caused me to attend the general meetings and take more interest in the doings of our committee.

More and more, in THESE POOR HANDS, the relations between management and men take on the form of a battle. Coombes's father-in-law is victimized after blacklegs are used to break a localized strike in which he (as a checkweigher) is involved, and he is unable to get work in the area for nearly five years. But Coombes recognizes that the solidarity of miners can never be automatic. Although during the 1921 lock-out the community pulls together in adversity, this unity is eroded in the aftermath of the dispute:

When all the miners were idle we felt a sort of companionship with one another. We were all fighting for a principle, and would begin work when it was decided. Then the others re-started work, and we were idle. We felt the bitterness of being unwanted. The hooters were blowing for others, not for us. They would have a pay on the weekend, but we would have none. I used to lie awake in the morning and listen, with despair in my heart, to the rattle of heavy boots on the streets when the other men went to work.

The colliery management prefer to employ men who live away from the mine (from Merthyr, Dowlais and Aberavon) because they are difficult to organize and are reluctant to attend trade union meetings. During the 1926 strike, blacklegs are imported to work the mine, and these *dregs of a large town* steal the local men's tools to add insult to injury. A few (*not a dozen*) local men join them, including Coombes's workmate Billy Ward. When work resumes there is tension underground until the blacklegs eventually drift away. A strong sense of righteous masculinity pervades the book, accentuated when, during lock-outs and periods of unemployment, Coombes has to seek financial assistance from the authorities of the Poor Law:

All the long shifts and the weeks without proper rest, all the dangers I had passed through and the dust I had swallowed, had gained me this much: that I had to go and beg for parish relief.

What makes such injustice all the harder to bear, whether it is meted out by the colliery management or by the state, is the fact that the miners must contend, in their work, not simply with dust, darkness and damp, but also with danger and dread. Death, whether actual or feared, is a constant presence in THESE POOR HANDS. Before he starts work Coombes speculates over the choice of grave-yards should he be killed underground, and listens to stories of explosions experienced by the landlord of his friend Jack. He notices the sober dress of families out and about on a Sunday afternoon:

when one has many responsibilities to meet it is wise to limit the clothing to dark colours, so that when the sad days come one is prepared – and those days come suddenly to mining families.

These premonitions are confirmed when fellow miner David Jones has his right foot sliced off by a stone falling from the roof, and is transformed immediately into 'Dai Peg'. Coombes tells this story in a restrained, understated manner, but spares little of the horror when his friend Jack Edwards, the main breadwinner in his family, is killed in front of his father:

a large stone had slid from the side and its sharp edge had caught Jack against the tram, almost severing the upper part of his body from the lower.

The low value assigned by the company to a miner's life is exposed by the fact that Jack's family receive only £18 in compensation for his death, whereas they valued a pit pony at £40. Jack's is but the first death in the book: two men are killed in shot-firing; a fifteen-year-old boy is crushed by stonefall, his body taken home covered with brattice-cloth and overcoats; and the penultimate chapter includes a reworking of the events that inspired 'Twenty Tons of Coal'. Here, the death of the character Hutch, like so many others, Coombes implies, was due to a shirking of the necessary safety precautions in favour of a hurried concentration on results above all else. Coombes has already observed that his first 'butty', John,

would not be kept in the mines to-day, because he was too

careful, too experienced, to rush his work and take the risks men are forced to do in the mines now.

The tension between careful work in which the skills of the craftsman could be expressed, and the rapid coal-getting that the management encourage is heightened by the arrival of coal-cutting machinery: *What a collier could do by working hard all day, this machine would accomplish in two minutes.* But

the drawback was in the added danger, because we could not hear the roof cracking, and with such a large undercut there was the likelihood of it falling any second.

When Coombes is appointed 'coal-cutter operator', this leads to further 'speed-up', with the operating team working sixteen hours a day: *We never knew when we would finish work. Every day was an emergency.* The saving grace of underground work, the only compensation one senses, is its comradeship, expressed vividly in Coombes's description of his relationship with Tommy Davies:

Tommy was a great worker. Hour after hour he would bang the heavy bottom mandril behind the slips of the coal. We learned to lift together automatically, to change our working positions to suit each other without saying a word, and to vary our jobs so that the change should give some rest. For some years we shared out troubles and joys, good weeks and bad, fears and ambitions – we were real 'butties'.

No reader of THESE POOR HANDS could doubt the physical strain of the miner's work, the injustices to which he is subjected, and the possibility of injury and death with which he must contend. The book's title was itself inspired by Coombes's contemplation of his own scarred and bruised flesh. Yet Coombes portrays his workmates not as Stakhanovite proletarians, but as men with flaws and foibles. There is sufficient humour to leaven the grim account of labour and exploitation, as when Coombes explains the dangers of the electricity used to power the coal-cutting machinery:

One man who was sitting across the cable happened to get on a live spot, and jumped up until his head hit the top six inches above him. He sat down again quickly, then jumped again and groaned.

'What's the matter, Fred?' we asked, very solicitously, although we knew he was sitting on a leaky part.

'Don't know, mun.' He was completely puzzled. 'I 'spects as it's them old rheumatics agen. Every time I puts my weight down I do get it summat awful.'

In the final chapter of THESE POOR HANDS Coombes describes a single, typical, underground shift. It starts with him *enjoying those last few minutes before I must change my clothes,* on the way to the mine. The work ahead, he dreads:

I have been lucky enough to avoid serious accident to myself over all these years, but I cannot check the feeling that some day I shall be just that important second too late when jumping back from a stone which is falling, or will be just a yard too near a tram when the rope snaps . . .

He also worries about the future of his family (*what may happen to the ones I leave behind*), then rushes to catch his bus where he meets his 'butty' Crush Williams. The shift proceeds, initially without incident. Coombes and Crush are set to work clearing a fall, stripped to their singlets:

56

It is squeezing all around. Stones that have been walled on the sides are crumbling to pieces because of the pressure; there is a continual crack-crack all about the place as timber breaks or the stones part into smaller divisions.

Breaking for food, a stone crashes down on the exact spot where Coombes had been working but a few minutes earlier. Shortly afterwards Crush is almost transfixed by a splitting piece of timber, but manages to escape with severe grazing. The shift ends:

'There,' Crush stated definitely, 'that's the end of another week. I'll have a look at a game this afternoon, and a couple of drinks after. Then we'll have a good dinner on Sunday, and I'll have a good sleep. When I wakes up it'll be near time to come to work, and another week-end 'ull be over.'

'Not much of a prospect, is it?' I asked.

'Course it ain't,' he agreed; 'but what else is there?'

'Not much, I know,' I answered; 'yet it could be a lot different.'

'Aye, I knows as it ought to be,' Crush said, 'but – '

At the nearest of the boilers a stoker walked across to a lever. He lifted his hand up, then pulled his watch from his waistcoat pocket.

'He's behind, as usual,' one of the waiting men complained.

Suddenly the stoker jerked his hand sharply downward and the hooter blared out. The crowd of men surged forward.

'There she goes,' Crush shouted; 'let's hop it.'

And we went, swiftly.

In this unorthodox but powerful way Coombes encapsulates the fundamental human message of his autobiography. The release and relief of the weekend lie ahead, but his life and that of those like him, could, and should, *be a lot different*. The fact that the narrative remains explicitly open-ended, rather than subject to the artificial closure to which so many autobiographers are forced to resort, reinforces this sense of future possibilities. Earlier in the book Coombes had written: *[I]f a man is sensitive and thinks about things, he must surely get to hate the injustice of it all*. Readers of THESE POOR HANDS were, and still are, inclined to agree.

VI

The extraordinary success of THESE POOR HANDS offered Coombes the possibility of leaving the coal industry to become a professional writer. Developments during the war years added to the opportunities open to him as, in addition to writing, his activities expanded (from October 1941) into radio broadcasting and writing scripts for documentary films. Coombes emerged as one of the miners' premier unofficial spokesmen, and as a leading campaigner for the establishment of a fairer society, his opinions and ideas sought by many. These were the years when, as one newspaper put it, *what with mining, writing and farming, he must be one of the busiest men in South Wales* (unattributed cutting, 'Scrapbook').

What remains so remarkable about Coombes is that, despite the surely powerful temptation to abandon the persistent physical danger, mental strain and relatively poor financial rewards of mining in favour of the career of a full-time writer, he remained securely grounded in the craft, class and society of the valley in which he lived. It was often suggested to him that he should change his calling, yet he chose not to, and instead, as the title of his 1957 dramatized autobiography for radio proudly and defiantly asserts, 'I Stayed a Miner'.

Coombes was dubious about making writing a full-time job. Mining held out the promise of a certain financial security which freelance writing did not: *if some day they won't publish what I write then I can tell them all right, I can still use the pick and shovel* ('I Stayed a Miner'). Coombes also had some measure of job satisfaction – *I enjoy my job and I want to stay with it for I find things that are interesting around me every day* ('Below the Tower') – and valued the camaraderie of his workmates. However, there were deeper reasons for his remaining a manual worker, which go to the heart of his purpose in writing, and which clarify his understanding of the nature of working-class writing itself. His continuing inspiration was to rectify what he felt was an overwhelming public ignorance of the nature of miners' lives, in and out of work. To do that effectively, he needed to remain amongst his work-mates:

The real history of the mines ought to be written by a man still at work underground. The dust should still be in his throat as he was writing – it seemed to me – then it would be authentic.

('A Miner's Record – I')

It is important to note that, for Coombes, it was not only the possession of direct experience of mining life that was crucial. He needed a continuing involvement: to leave the coal industry would signal an immediate loss of credentials and, as he informed Gwyn Jones in 1941, *I believe I would lose intimacy also.* Coombes remained steadfast in this belief, even though the strain of fulfilling so many obligations clearly told. On 12 November 1941, A. L. Lloyd, a PICTURE POST photographer who had got to know Coombes well, wrote to him to express his concern that:

you didn't look very well . . . you should be careful not to try to do too much. It can eventually play hell with your writing as well as your health as one sees with people like poor Lewis Jones. And while I thoroughly sympathise with your feeling that if you give up work in the colliery you may lose a certain authenticity, I feel that you possibly overestimate this. After all, it's a milieu about which you already know all there is to know. And socially you wouldn't be isolated in any way from mining life, even if you did give it up.

Coombes, however, continued to insist that *a writer should stay amongst his people and live the life he describes in his words* (NEATH GUARDIAN, 29 January 1943). He justified his views at greater length in 'The Working Class Writer':

If you, a working-class writer, leave the valleys and live for one year away from them . . . their lives and thoughts will fade from among your closest memories, and in that interval many fresh problems will have arisen, which you know nothing about. Many a working-class writer has been ruined by going away from the only life he knows anything about, and trying to live on his mental capital. You won't catch me leaving my valley.

Another important justification for Coombes maintaining his link with mining was that, without it, he would lose the source of much of his material, thus committing a form of creative suicide. In 'I Stayed a Miner', Mary suggests to Coombes that following the acceptance of THESE POOR HANDS and its adoption by the Left Book Club he can now afford to give up work underground. Coombes responds with a typically down-to-earth metaphor:

Not likely. I know mining life inside out and that is the special value of my writing. If you are in a desert and dying for lack of water you know and can describe what a terrible thing thirst

can be. Unless you have suffered you cannot properly under-
stand. For the same reason my every day experience of mining is
my most valuable asset.

Coombes never seriously contemplated moving away from the identity of 'miner-writer' that, in his mid-forties, he had forged for himself. Moreover, he developed his own philosophy of what it meant to be a working-class writer, expressed most clearly in his article 'Below the Tower', his contribution to a wider debate on contemporary writing in Britain that had been stimulated by Virginia Woolf's 'The Leaning Tower' (FOLIOS OF NEW WRITING, Autumn 1940).

In 'The Leaning Tower' Woolf analysed trends in literature in Britain between the wars. The tower concerned was the privileged position of the middle-class writer who had been educated at public school and university. Woolf argued that there was a necessary connection between the education and social status of the writer and the excellence of their creative work. However, she considered that, since the 1920s, there had emerged a group of writers who, in embracing the political left (and often contributing to NEW WRITING), had reacted against their class, status and privilege. But although these writers had politicized their writing, to Woolf they remained privileged, unable to descend from the tower, for such a descent would render them unable to write. So the tower might be leaning to the left, but it remained a tower.

Coombes was one of three writers (Louis MacNiece and John Upward were the others) whom John Lehmann asked to respond to Woolf. His contribution begins with him stating that he writes in order to express his disagreement with some of Woolf's views, and these points of contention structure the text. First, Coombes rejects Woolf's belief that at the lower levels of society the working class and the poor belonged to separate classes: *there is no margin between the two.* He argues that the security of manual workers is precarious, owing to the possibility of loss of work through illness, injury or unemployment, and the consequent likelihood of destitution. As for writers from other classes, they look down on this single class

with an interest . . . sharpened by the fear that if ever their tower should collapse they will have to join the crowd below and so may get their clothes soiled.

In turn the working class is, with good reason, wary of the classes above it.

Coombes contends that *if we are to survive,* the gap between the classes has to be bridged. The means by which this can be achieved

is the worker who is also a writer. He is almost the only one who can connect both sides and I feel he should be encouraged because, for good or evil, he is going to play a most important role in the future of our lives and our literature.

Coombes proceeds to discuss the nature and experiences of working-class writers in order to rectify the lack of consideration given to them by Woolf. He acknowledges that Woolf was correct in her belief that the canon of English literature would scarcely suffer if those works written by members of the working class had never been produced. But this was only part of the matter. Admittedly working-class writing was not yet strong, but it needed encouragement not criticism:

for the most part it is still like an alarmed infant, whimpering at finding itself in strange company and fearing that it may be cuffed before being sent back to its home.

Coombes continues by upbraiding Woolf for not having displayed sufficient awareness of the obstacles the budding working-class writer had to overcome. Very likely with his own experiences fresh in his mind he writes that

it seems that every door is shut against him, that he has set himself a most hopeless task, and that writing must be in every pulse of his being if he can survive and express himself at last.

That said, the growth in working-class writing in itself indicates that the working class is no longer prepared to accept a system based on injustice and tyranny, and that education – *as well as opportunity* – must be *made free and equal for all.*

For Coombes, working-class writers, despite their problems, have the advantage over writers of 'The Leaning Tower', in that *the material for our shaping is very close to our hands.* Writers with an expensive education cannot see this material, but working-class writers *are in the ant heap and do not view it from a distance.* Coombes argues against Woolf's suggestion that *it is death for a writer to throw away his capital; to be forced to earn his living in a mine or a factory.* Although, for a middle-class writer, such a life might *upset all his ideas*:

It is just as surely the creative end of a working class writer if he leaves his own sphere; he has grown into it and the labour is part of his being. If one accepts the statement by Virginia Woolf as it is written it means that no one who works at manual labour can ever hope to be a writer. She may not have thought of it that way but the result must be so. What else can it be?

In 'Below the Tower' Coombes offers a spirited defence of working-class writers. He also expresses his disappointment that middle-class intellectuals and writers found it necessary to be aloof and superior. He ends by stating his conviction that working-class writers need their literary counterparts in the upper ranks of society, as much as the latter need the former. Explaining that he is a capable violinist but is not inspired by a symphony concert, he admits that it is because he has *not been properly trained to the beauty of great music*. And:

It is the same with the classics of literature. I know they should be enjoyed yet I cannot get the full flavour. I want those from the Leaning Tower to come down and teach me what I lack.

'Below the Tower' is less a theoretical critique of Woolf's position, and more a defence of working-class writing that comes straight from the heart. Coombes adopts the broad parameters of Woolf's analysis, but also succeeds in exposing the class-based assumptions and prejudices that he feels have blinded her to the value of working-class writing. 'Below the Tower' is a forceful statement of Coombes's own *raison d'être* as a 'miner-writer', revealing his strength of belief and developing self-confidence in this role. As he writes towards the end of the article, *I am an adventurer in literature, but my step is getting firm and my hand is quite strong.*

VII

The outbreak of the Second World War had, initially, a positive impact on the fortunes of the south Wales coal industry. Rearmament and the exigencies of the war economy resulted in an increased demand for coal and its workers, unemployment eased and wages rose. Coombes himself noticed the improvement locally – *the most obvious sign of the war is that we are working full-time and that lost days from work do not trouble us any more* – although he was unconvinced that the colliery management were entering into the co-operative wartime spirit:

We seem to be plastered with new problems at our colliery and it seems every advantage of the times is being taken. Customs are broken and wage rates reduced so often that we have to meet two and three nights a week. Now that strikes are not allowed we have hardly any power and the management take full advantage of it. War seems, to them, an opportunity for robbing our men in every way under the excuse of patriotism. One official told me that when Hitler won there would be an end of this humbugging with the Federation. I answered that if Hitler did win there might be many things on the company's side that might be altered too.
('The War Diary of a Welsh Miner', 1939–41)

The demand for coal was so high that the colliers' August holidays were cancelled, but come autumn 1940, *there is gloomy talk in this area, miners are having notice and it is said that some collieries are closing down.* In part this was due to the impact of the fall of France, which led to a collapse in the export market, particularly for anthracite coal. Coombes's colliery, producing largely for the internal market, was given brief respite, only to close in November, with the excuse that the railways were *'acting the goat'*. Coombes's personal experiences of lengthy delays at the labour exchange, and sneers and jibes from the clerks, fuelled his frustration. He observed *men, women and children scratching for coal in the tips,* and families with empty grates, yet the mountain was *so full of coal that it crops out to the surface*. The obscenity of capitalist inefficiency was not lost on Coombes:

in this area where the coal dust kills men every day we are ourselves short of coal . . . I was so blazingly bitter about the whole muddle and the meanness that I sat down and wrote a letter to a great national weekly – with over a million circulation – to explain the whole situation as I saw it.

The *great national weekly* was PICTURE POST, whose assistant editor, Charles Fenby, replied on 28 November 1940, hoping that Coombes *might help us to express in human terms what has long been in our minds,* namely a discussion of 'peace aims'; *an outline of the better Britain we want to build up.* Most of this *outline,* including plans for better social security, education and health services, and improvements in local government, housing and town planning would be drafted by experts, but

we do want to get somebody who is closer to reality than the politician, publicist, doctor etc., & I do feel that you are the man to state the aspirations of the masses of people.

The result, 'This is the Problem', appeared in the 'Plan for Britain' issue of PICTURE POST (10, No. 1) on 4 January 1941.

'This is the Problem' is, according to the byline, *something about life to-day, as it looks to me and my mates.* It is headed by a photograph of Coombes, together with son Peter and their dog Sam, overlooking the Vale of Neath, *scarred by colliery refuse,* the mines *idle in the midst of war.*

Coombes begins the article by referring to his days on the land, and to his decision to migrate to work in the mines. Now, however, in the midst of a war, he is idle, as is Peter: *the country does not want his skill or his labour.* He is quite explicit in blaming the war and its attendant economic misery upon the country's ruling class:

More than half of my mates saw what was coming when Spain was sacrificed, and we collected from our small earnings to help what we knew was the first line of the defence; then Czechoslovakia was betrayed and a moan of sorrow went through the mines. Since then, we have always wondered whether they who governed us were wilfully blind or incredibly stupid.

Those blunders have finished for ever the tradition of a class that was born to govern . . .

Coombes asks for a new appreciation of the manual worker in the future, for *great changes in the men and women who run this country,* and for *new ideas and new methods.* The 'peace aim' he wants above all is security:

security against war and exploitation, by man or country. And what I ask for ourselves should be granted to the whole world.

'This is the Problem' is illustrated with poignant photographs of miners picking a tip for waste coal, of Coombes walking past a row of empty coal trucks and of him with his grandchildren. The last caption asks *So will there be any place for the grandsons?* In the remainder of the issue the 'experts', including Thomas Balogh, A. D. Lindsay, Julian Huxley and J. B. Priestley, tried to provide a positive answer to Coombes's closing question.

'Plan for Britain' was an enormous success, arousing more interest and producing a bigger correspondence than any issue in the history of PICTURE POST (Sir Tom Hopkinson, letter to THE TIMES, 8 January 1980). Coombes himself received 'piles of letters' (letter to Gwyn Jones, 15 January 1941), and his contribution was marked out for particular praise by Lord Addison, Sean O'Casey and Lord Cecil. At a subsequent meeting held in London in February, Coombes spoke before his fellow contributors and interested persons on the subject of 'What we mean by a full life', drawing the tribute from Honor Balfour (letter to Coombes, 28 February 1941) that

[i]t is very rarely that any of us has the opportunity of hearing such a sincere talk, and one so full of observation, knowledge and human sympathy.

At home, however, Coombes reported that he had *piles of complaints that I was not talking to this one or that one in this street or that street when I was snapped,* and that when collecting the paper he was

so long delayed by people who insisted on talking about the pictures and the letter that I was away four hours – and the fire was out when I got home.

('The War Diary of a Welsh Miner')

In THE LIFE WE WANT, the 1944 pamphlet that Coombes co-authored with Lord Meston, he drew upon similar themes and recycled a number of the points made in 'This is the Problem'. Officially published by the Liberal Party, the pamphlet disclaimed 'any bias of political partisanship', being concerned instead to advocate a broad progressive agenda including an attack on poverty and ignorance, and the championing of both full employment and welfare state complete with a better, state-financed, health service. Coombes concluded:

War has brought us all nearer to one another. Many people have seen and lived through things during the war which they might never have experienced otherwise. This is all to the good. For it is only through a liberal tolerance towards the less fortunate and an unselfish willingness to sacrifice on the part of the rest that we shall achieve the new kind of brotherhood that is the only thing that can make this war worthwhile

Coombes's idealism, the simplicity of his vision of a future in which everyone would be accorded their worth without prejudice, and in which they would enjoy a full range of educational and cultural opportunities, undoubtedly struck a chord with the mood of wartime Britain. But it was the much greater volume of his output on coal mining, dominated by a concern as to how that giant industry might be restructured to the benefit of all, that continued to characterize his writing throughout the war and peace decade of the 1940s.

VIII

Between September 1939 and the end of 1945, B. L. Coombes wrote at least nineteen factual articles that were published in literary, geographical and political magazines including The Listener, The New Statesman, Fortnightly, and New Writing and Daylight. Of these, fourteen were concerned directly with coal mining. In the same period he wrote two short books on the same subject: Those Clouded Hills (1944) and Miners Day (1945). As with Coombes's other writings, there is often overlap or duplication between many of the works, but the books are quite distinct in tenor and ambition, and merit separate treatment. Although, occasionally, they touch on similar themes to those treated in I am a Miner and These Poor Hands, they have an added aura of authority gleaned from those works' earlier success. In writing Those Clouded Hills and Miners Day, Coombes was in no doubt that he had an important message to communicate, and that he had both the necessary means and the opportunity.

Those Clouded Hills was written in the autumn of 1943 whilst Coombes was recovering from *a nasty knock underground*. It was published in March 1944, in both Britain and the United States, and was subsequently chosen as a 'literary ambassador' by the 'Books Across the Sea' Club. Dedicated *to the world's workers*, it is a documentary, almost synchronic, account of the coal industry, and of the work of the miner, in which Coombes, as author-narrator,

remains sparing with the personal anecdotes that
had been used to such effect in his 1939 publications.
Yet, as G. Illtyd Lewis commented in WALES (4, No. 6,
Winter 1945):

*the book is far more than a Fabian-like pamphlet on an
industrial problem . . . it has in its wealth of intimate
description a human interest which supersedes the cold
arguments of the pamphleteer, and which recommends it as a
piece of vital reading where a mere pamphlet or treatise would
never penetrate.*

Coombes's success in rendering his industry – his
world – transparent to the non-specialist, is reliant
upon the authenticity that he brings and em-
phasizes, in his persona as a working miner. As he
explains in the introduction:

*I want to take you into a hidden world, into the dark
underground where I spend one-third of my time. You see, if
you watch a man ploughing a field or building part of a house,
you gain some knowledge of what skill he has and what energy
he must expend. It may not be difficult to discover how he is
paid and how he and his family live.*

*With us in the mining industry it is far different. We work out
of sight beneath the ground in conditions which are difficult to
describe, and quite impossible to imagine.*

Coombes is, as in his previous books, at pains to
emphasize the skill of the miner (*our lives depend on
it*), the *unnatural conditions* and danger in which
mining must be carried out, and the peculiar bond
that is shared by miners but which sets them apart
from the rest of society. Coal, of course, is of *immense
value: In this time of battle and mechanical warfare it has
been found the most essential – next to food – of our*

productions and this, Coombes suggests, has led to greater public awareness of and interest in the miner's case. Coombes's objective, as *one of the workers*, is to state that case *simply and fairly*:

I want to leave the past – the bitter past – behind, and to show you the present mining position as I see it each day; and after that to sketch very briefly the future, and that happier and brighter era to which we are all looking and for which we must all work. I'll take you over the colliery screens to see the coal being treated; over the yards where large stocks of material must always be maintained; past the great engine houses and under the steel arches to where the water and rushing air current meets you. We'll see the different kinds of coal, the various seams and methods of working, the grades of mining workmen and the young boys coming eager-eyed to this strange world. We'll go out again into daylight and watch the men getting paid, the compensation doctors and their methods; the injured and diseased miners; the homes and families to which my mates take their pay, and to which we have sometimes to carry their broken bodies.

Coombes, perhaps conscious of his unusual skill as a writer, feels the need at this point to remind his readers:

that it is not a visiting journalist who is writing – looking on these strange humans as a scientist studies an ant hill – but a miner, or a miner writer if you like, who knows the life backwards and is content to stay working with his mates.

He proclaims his intention to be fair in his judgements:

the managements who face us across the disputes table are sometimes composed of humane men, who try to be as generous as the system under which they work will allow

– but the sentence with which he ends the book's introduction leaves no doubt as to where Coombes's essential sympathies lie:

Of the coalowners – I know little about them; I have never seen one, and in any case they are wealthy enough to find their own chronicler.

Although six of the eight chapters of THOSE CLOUDED HILLS are, ostensibly, politically neutral documentary, they throb with a sense of injustice and with an imperative that the post-war world should right the miners' wrongs. The tone is set in the first few pages, when, in the process of explaining the characteristics and qualities of the different types of coal, Coombes pauses to illustrate the effect anthracite dust has on the miner's lungs, and advises the reader to *rub some grit in a silk handkerchief, from that you will get an idea of the meaning of anthracosis.* Reviewing the recent history of the coal industry, he observes that even during the Great War miners felt that their interests were not being looked after, and that when the Sankey Commission reported in 1919, there was a *feeling that we were at last to have 'a square deal'.* As far as Coombes is concerned the verdict was clear, but somehow *the condemned have avoided retribution.* Consequently the inter-war decades have not been pleasant:

That period has been one of deceit after deceit, frustration after frustration, mounting into a crescendo of bitterness that may slacken with the passing years, but will never be forgotten. The children in mining areas knew that their fathers were real men, their mothers equal to any women in the land, and yet they saw them treated as if they encumbered the earth. They have decided that the agony they saw in the lives of their loved parents shall

74

never be their lot. If ever the official mind has shown itself brutal and inefficient it is in the handling of the miners and their problems.

For all the hardship and humiliation of those years, Coombes feels that *there was a spirit amongst us that could not be crushed, and the mills of retribution are grinding out in these days.* There must be hope in the future, a future in which coal will remain a vital product.

Even Coombes's apparently straightforward descriptions of what he sees around him are shot through with symbolic meaning. Observing the trucks being loaded with coal on their way to distant markets, Coombes reflects that the names that are painted on their sides – Oxcroft, Sheepcotes and Fernlea – *seem almost blasphemous in these surroundings.* The aesthetic discomfort of the besmirching of a rural idyll is as nothing, however, compared with the miners' feelings when

we look with tightened chests on a word like Gresford, and think of those other miners who went in to that shift that has kept them forever buried in the depths with the coal.

Once away from the *intense blackness* of the underground, Coombes details the role of the miners' lodge, giving an impression of dedicated and often thankless service by committeemen, concerned above all with the day-to-day problems of their members, and vigilant in maintaining their rights. Coombes is sceptical of the effectiveness of the system of joint (he calls it *piebald*) control in the wartime industry, with its pit-production committees. In the future he believes there will be one of two alternatives: either all mines will be absorbed into a united *soulless* combine or there will be nationalization:

the only hope of a better mining future . . . under which the mines will be worked for the good of all and the miners can use their skill and enthusiasm to the human limit, knowing that their future is secure and their efforts are making life brighter and easier for the other millions of workers in the world.

In the last two chapters of THOSE CLOUDED HILLS Coombes raises his gaze from the mine, looking to the wider society. *In the future,* he writes, *we must get up on the mountains,* and advocates the building of semi-detached houses to replace the terraces on the valley floor, making *these slopes useful again as homes for people.* To escape the dust for the mountain air, smallholdings could be provided, on which calves, pigs and poultry could be kept. *This scheme will cost money and manpower,* he admits, but:

In the past manpower has rusted on the corners of mining streets and it may come that way again. Millions of pounds are being spent daily for less beneficial and lasting things than this.

One way to finance the project, he suggests, *would be to charge those folk who have made riches from underneath this land.* He ends the book abruptly, linking the possibilities of a new harmony between land and people to the brighter prospects of a nationalized coal industry:

There is blood on the coal, there will always be blood on the coal, but we feel that blood should be shed for the mass who are our kin, not for the enrichment of a few who have battened on our pain in the past.

Coombes, moving in 1941 from Oak Lodge to Ynysgron, a small mountain farm of sixty acres at Cwmgwrach, had already followed the advice he gave in THOSE CLOUDED HILLS. Once there he wrote that he was *like an eagle – or a crow – perched above the valley and the villages, so I can see and even hear everything that goes on below.* It was whilst at Ynysgron that Coombes began MINERS DAY, eventually published as a Penguin Special in December 1945. MINERS DAY is perhaps best understood as THESE POOR HANDS with the autobiographical narrative removed, for it is essentially a contemporary, observational account of mining life and work, much in the style of the conversational passages of the earlier text, spiced with social comment and political argument. The title is a misnomer, for this is not an account of a day in the life of a miner, but almost a collection of sketches, written over many months during 1944 and the first part of 1945.

MINERS DAY opens with Coombes on his way to work, of which he writes:

I am in it every day. In some ways repelled by what I see and feel, yet in other aspects enjoying the battle with the inside of the mountain; but most especially happy to be a good comrade for most of these men who are moving alongside me now.

These men – Benjy, Steve, Crush, Hermit and George, to name but a few – share Coombes's shift and the dangers that come with it. In the course of the book, brief character sketches and humorous anecdotes relieve (for both author and reader) the depressing yet undeniably human accounts of those disabled and dying from lung diseases brought about by the inhalation of coal dust. Two miners – Dan and Tom – were sketched for MINERS DAY by Isabel Alexander: both died before the book was published (letter to Jack Lindsay, 7 December 1945). Occasionally Coombes breaks off to comment on the pay disputes that bedevilled the miners during the latter stages of the war, or to explain how he passes his weekends, with newspaper, magazine, book and radio, or his Wednesday afternoons, visiting Neath market in the company of other rural migrants. More so than in any other of his writings, Coombes emerges in MINERS DAY as a union activist, even chairing a pithead meeting. Despite the fact that reconstruction and change is on the horizon, he remains angry at the way in which the miners are viewed by the general public, *an encumbrance* when coal is not needed, *but when coal is needed they are treated as useful citizens, both by the masters and the country.* Sitting in Victoria Gardens, Neath, after attending an X-ray examination, he watches the townspeople pass by and expresses his sense of estrangement:

This was normal life to them, the only way they understood. What did they know of roof falls, or stiff working coal, or men who gasped as they breathed? What did they care while the sun shone and the world was bright? Yet nearly three-quarters of a million men – my mates – were shut away from that sun. Their normal life was about them then, in a crushing darkness with sweat running down their backs to make their singlets like a wet cloth. Men straining to rip out the compressed sunlight which had been stored in the heart of creation uncounted centuries before; and which to a greater or a lesser degree affects all our lives and our national prosperity.

MINERS DAY ends with a plea for a new approach to social problems, a 'wise control' to use the resources of the land (below and above ground) for the common good, instead of leaving coal in the seams, letting farms go derelict, and allowing human talents to be dissipated in unemployment and idleness. The system that has produced these effects, writes Coombes, *does not deserve to endure – it cannot last.*

IX

We have passed through the dark years. The years when nights were black periods after fearful and tortured days. Periods when our lives and our future seemed almost without hope. Then, so unexpectedly that we could scarcely believe it, the clouds of European war and slaughter passed from our lives. Close behind that lifting came the sunshine and brightness of a happening which has altered the feeling of our whole lives. Something has come to our country, a change of heart which many hoped and prayed for all through their thinking hours, but which seemed almost impossible of realisation. Socialism has come – in our time.
(NEATH GUARDIAN, 3 August 1945)

B. L. Coombes gave a euphoric welcome to the Labour Party's electoral victory and first majority government. Although never a party member, and always willing to find good in the programmes of other parties (the Conservatives excepted), he admitted later that *during the first half of my life I was almost a fanatic for Socialism* ('Home on the Hill'). He attended Labour Party meetings as a lodge delegate (the miners' union being affiliated to Labour) and was a keen supporter of its proposal to nationalize the mines. In fact, although Coombes had taken a wide-ranging view of politics and policy in 'This is the Problem' and THE LIFE WE WANT, and would again in later life in his regular column in the NEATH GUARDIAN, during the second half of the 1940s he concentrated most of his intellectual energy in setting out his blueprint for a nationalized coal industry, and in reacting to the realities of public ownership after 1 January 1947.

Coombes was in no doubt that nationalization was necessary. In his article 'The Miner and Nationalization' in FORTNIGHTLY (951, March 1946) he explained that, to younger miners in particular:

the coal owners and their representatives were as much an enemy as the nations who had fought against us. They had mishandled the industry, they had caused the misery and insecurity in their homes and the lives of their parents, and such power and control must go for ever.

To replace this, Coombes, like the National Union of Mineworkers, advocated the implementation of the 'Miners' Charter', a twelve-point series of demands for better safety and training provisions, the combating of the dangers of mechanization and dust, an improvement in medical services and the handling of compensation cases, a new wage structure, a shorter working week, longer paid holidays, enhanced pensions, the provision of work for ill and disabled miners, and better housing conditions (NEATH GUARDIAN, January–April 1947, *passim*). He collaborated with Jack Lindsay in writing the play FACE OF COAL: A PROVOCATIVE DOCUMENTARY, which appeared at the Scala Theatre in London in 1946. FACE OF COAL explored the inefficiencies and injustices of private enterprise via the story of a Bevin Boy named Jack Smith, a Londoner who comes to work in a south Wales mining valley during the Second World War, and the play culminates in a strong backing for the 'Miners' Charter'. For reasons seemingly unconnected with the quality of the play, it ran for only a week.

When nationalization did take place, Coombes's reaction was enthusiastic. In his article 'Their Hour

has Struck' (DAILY WORKER, 2 January 1947) he wrote
of being underground as the New Year dawned:

*Usually we pause for just those few seconds when the old
surrenders to the new, but this year we were conscious that
much more than a year was passing into history.*

*This midnight of December 31 was taking with it the end of a
system – a system which had killed itself by its greed.*

When the night shift emerged from the mine

*we did not meet men coming up the incline. They were massed on
the road outside the Pithead baths. A wintry sun peeped over the
mountain to see what was going on as the announcement of
Vesting was made. All over the land, at the same time, miners
listened at nearly two thousand collieries. A new phase in our life
had started. A great experiment in industry was to be tried out.*

('Home on the Hill')

Coombes had high hopes for the nationalized industry. However, he realized that, in many respects,
the personnel and style of colliery management,
which he had expended so much energy in criticiz-
ing, remained largely unchanged. Equally he felt that
the miners had a responsibility to make the new
system work (*with new privileges come greater responsibilities*, he wrote in 'You are being Watched', COAL, 1,
No. 4, August 1947). Reviewing the progress made in
the first year of public ownership in 'And now – the
first year of Nationalisation in South Wales is summed up' (COAL, 1, No. 9, January 1948), he acknowledged that his own coalfield was one where

*the bitterness of industrial conflict had torn its deepest, and the
gap between management and men was widest . . . We held*

bitter memories here that could not be understood even by miners working in other parts of the coalfields.

Yet, *the doubt is slowly easing,* and Coombes recognized that there had been improvements in the length of the working week, safety, canteen provision, pithead baths and welfare work. Slowly, however, he became more disillusioned, writing in the NEATH GUARDIAN (21 October 1949) that

right from the start the wrong men were put in control over the nationalised industry . . . the bright hopes of nationalisation are fading, leaving an embittered industry where so much might have been done with the new idea fostered by new men.

In his article 'A Miner Considers' (FORTNIGHTLY, 1013, May 1951) he argued that the miners had lost their enthusiasm for nationalization, and that some even argued that it was worse than private ownership: all in all, *nowadays the National Coal Board seems to have no more friends among the miners than did the colliery owners in the past.* Coombes did not think this state of affairs was simply the fault of the management: the miners' union were also to blame for not being prepared to take a more active role in controlling and managing the industry. Towards the end of the 1950s, he reflected that

the miners and their union were like an army whose opponents have retreated but have no trained men ready to lead them in the new country and the fresh type of battle.

Altogether, he concluded, *it is a rather depressing tale of an ideal gone sour* ('Home on the Hill').

Coombes's progressive disillusionment with nationalization was mirrored by his reaction to the success of the Labour Party at both parliamentary and local government levels. Socialism, he felt, had become respectable, a vehicle for careerists rather than for principled men. He was puzzled by Labour's foreign policy during the late 1940s, and particularly by the fact that it was supported by the Conservatives. This did not prevent him from preferring Labour governments to Conservative ones, nor from acknowledging the real advances in what he termed 'security' for ordinary working people that the welfare state and full employment had brought; but he despaired at the threat of nuclear war. His last publication to reach a national audience, his winning entry in the DAILY MIRROR competition of 1955, proclaimed the need for international friendship. All in all, Coombes suffered from a certain redundancy of purpose after nationalization, as the urgent evangelical edge of his earlier work as a 'miner-writer' under monopoly capitalism was not easily refocused in the new era of public ownership, full employment and the welfare state, and the reading world was no longer so eager for his brand of 'proletarian truth'.

X

The 1950s were a difficult time for Bert and Mary Coombes, as they were plagued by injury, ill-health and disappointment at having to give up farming. In autumn 1945 the proceeds from his writings had enabled Coombes, Mary and son Peter to move from Ynysgron Farm to the much larger Nantyfedwen Farm near Onllwyn. On top of all his other commitments, farming the new home's 160 acres demanded a colossal effort, especially as the Coombes family had also set up a milk round, providing produce for nearby collieries and villages. As time wore on, and as Peter left the family home, Nantyfedwen became increasingly difficult to maintain. Then, in 1954 or 1955, Coombes received a serious *smack in the back* underground, the last in the series of injuries he suffered at work. This caused him much pain (he had to wear a steel waistcoat thereafter) and necessitated numerous visits to medical boards. It quickly brought an end to his connection with the industry whose nature and problems he had dissected and disseminated for so long, forcing him to retire on a disability pension after having worked underground for over forty years. Mary, who had never enjoyed good health, was also a frequent visitor to hospital, enduring a series of operations from around this time. It quickly became an impossibility to look after Nantyfedwen, and consequently they sold all its stock and land *except three acres so we can walk around freely and keep a few poultry*. Late in life, Mary recalled that this was a bitter blow:

Looking back I often wonder how we did it all, Bert working by night and having very little sleep, me taking milk around and doing all the house-work, apart from turning hay sometimes for days if it rained. Sometimes it was heart-breaking for both of us. I would pitch while Bert would load. I could not stand on anything moving, yes, we worked together in everything. I enjoyed every minute of it and when the time came to give it up I thought the bottom of my world had fallen through. I was taken ill and had to go from hospital to hospital and at the same time Bert injured his back so it was hopeless to try and carry on. . . . It is sad to see things being sold and it upset us very much at the time.

('My Life from Childhood')

These adverse circumstances might well have deterred a less determined writer, but it is a tribute to Coombes's energy that he continued to write extensively throughout the 1950s, producing an unpublished autobiography and novel, and radio scripts for the Welsh Home Service and the Light Programme. Yet, despite this sustained creativity, it is equally true that Coombes was now enjoying only a fraction of the status and fame that had been his during the 1940s.

His radio broadcasts of the 1950s were dominated by mining themes, particularly descriptions of life underground and of the dangers that miners faced, although other topics were explored. The feature 'The Vale of Neath' was transmitted in September 1950, drawing heavily on his published articles on the same subject in GEOGRAPHICAL MAGAZINE and WALES, and indicating the extent to which most of his later works relied on the re-examination or even repetition of tried and trusted themes. There were four other broadcasts in the late 1950s, including the plays 'Eight-Pointed Star' (June 1957) which described the work of the St John Ambulance in the coal industry, and 'All Roads Blocked' (April 1960), in which miners are trapped underground after a roof fall. In 1957 Coombes wrote 'I Stayed a Miner', described as

an autobiographical study which recalls his struggle to achieve recognition and shows how his work and the comradeship of his mates underground provided him with first hand material and the inspiration to shape it into words.

By 1959 Coombes had also completed a second autobiography, 'Home on the Hill', which remained unpublished, and a similar fate befell a full-length novel, 'The Singing Sycamore', also written during the 1950s.

A key factor in Coombes's failure as a novelist may have been the relentless workload to which he subjected himself: as a full-time miner, part-time small farmer and regular contributor to all manner of journals and papers. He told Gwyn Jones in 1941 that he had had two enquiries about synopses for novels and was *especially keen on novel writing but find it hard to get time*. Fitting *forty-eight hours' work into each day*, he wrote in the NEATH GUARDIAN (13 July 1945), was how he managed, but this sort of intense activity may not have lent itself to the large-scale enterprise of a novel. Writing about his direct experience may have been simpler and easier than working with complex plot lines and deeper characterization. That said, and whatever his other qualities, perhaps Coombes did not possess all the attributes necessary to write full-length fiction. The surviving manuscript of 'The Singing Sycamore' and the extant sections of 'Castell Vale' suggest that he was happier with descriptive scene-setting than with narrative drive, and although his works of fiction contain memorable passages of acutely observed writing, their impact as novels is limited. Perhaps much is revealed by his comment in 'The Working-Class Writer' that when writing a novel *you can ramble a bit.*

Coombes was not completely ignored by the public eye during the last twenty-five years of his life, occasionally receiving acclaim and recognition. In 1950 he won a prize at Caerphilly National Eisteddfod for an essay on safety in mines. Five years later he won the DAILY MIRROR's literary competition on the theme of international friendship, being chosen out of 6,000 writers to attend a conference in Hamburg to meet with writers from eight countries. (He also subsequently won first prize for the best account of the visit submitted by the participating writers.) Between 1957 and 1960 he was successful in the Arthur Markham Memorial Competition (a competition for manual workers at a coal mine, or persons who had been injured when so employed) on three occasions, following on from his successes in 1943 and 1947. In 1963, in what he regarded as a *golden moment,* the National Union of Mineworkers (South Wales Area) presented him with a miniature miner's lamp as a tribute to his *outstanding contributions to working-class literature.* This was the first time the union had made a presentation to a miner-writer. Coombes wrote in the NEATH GUARDIAN (11 October 1963) that the honour *moved me greatly* and that the reception he had been given at the presentation had touched him far more than any he had had, either for FACE OF COAL at the Scala Theatre, or during his more recent visit to Germany. Finally, in

1972, he was unexpectedly granted a £250 award by the Royal Literary Fund in recognition of his work, a sum which supplemented the small pension he had been receiving from the Society of Authors (to which he had been elected in 1948) since the late 1950s.

After 1960, Coombes's literary output dwindled to his weekly column for the NEATH GUARDIAN. Beyond his immediate area, he effectively disappeared from public view. It is perhaps fitting that, given his local 'rootedness', this was the commitment he retained when all his other creative interests were abandoned. Indeed his dedication and consistency in writing for his local newspaper are quite remarkable.

He first wrote columns for the NEATH GUARDIAN in late 1940 and early 1941, and then from March 1944 until nearly the end of his life, rarely missing a week in all that time. Over the years he wrote on a wide range of issues, impressive in their diversity. Though naturally matters relating to mining achieved a great deal of attention, other topics he discussed included capital punishment and international relations, the beneficial effect of cider and, with great regularity, the changing nature of the countryside. His columns varied in nature and tone, being often anecdotal, reminiscent and nostalgic; at other times, being commentaries on local events and places, or on political affairs and social matters. In passing they contained much autobiographical material. Christopher Baggs, in his perceptive analysis of Coombes's wartime columns ('A "war-time mirror to Welsh life"? B. L. Coombes and the NEATH GUARDIAN', MORGANNWG, 34, 1990), has suggested that Coombes deliberately focused his articles on two main areas: first, *those topics which he knew would find resonance within his local readers . . . and with which he was also thoroughly conversant,* and interspersed with these were

others that set Coombes apart, his own unique interests, largely cultural, but still acceptable to and comprehensible by his readership as they are almost always linked to Wales and things Welsh.

Thus the issues and problems that Coombes dealt with were *typical of the difficulties and worries concerning the man on the Neath omnibus.* Baggs's analysis can profitably be extended to the columns Coombes wrote between the end of the war and 1971.

Throughout this very large body of writing – it amounts to nearly 1,500 items – Coombes reveals himself as a keen observer of human reactions and behaviour, and of the changing tempo of the natural world. What is equally evident is that he was willing to formulate and express a wide range of opinions, albeit with varying degrees of success. Many of his columns correspond to his own vision of what a local newspaper should be, as suggested in his column of 24 February 1956:

The main attraction of a local paper is its resemblance to a long talk, or a lengthy letter from home, to the many who have gone away yet still saving bitter-sweet memories of the old places and the people left behind. Such intimate news always pulls at the emotions and recreates past pleasures.

Coombes's NEATH GUARDIAN articles, as Baggs also correctly points out:

reveal a writer with a much broader spectrum of interests and a wider ability than he is generally given credit for from his best known works.

Mary Coombes died on 3 July 1970, and her loss was a deep blow to her husband. A fortnight after Mary's death Coombes wrote a touching tribute to her in the NEATH GUARDIAN, a good example of the way Coombes often used writing to ease his pain or anger. From this point on, until the end of his life, Coombes experienced intense feelings of isolation and loneliness. In July 1971 he wrote to Bob Langdon of the local St John Ambulance:

My sight is good and my hearing excellent, my weak spot is the legs as I cannot walk far without resting and I never learned to drive a car, a point I regret now. We live [in] a nice place with a large garden – which I cannot handle much now . . . As I am here by myself I often think about the old times, and the miners from Banwen often sit outside and chat but they are not the ones I worked and lived with . . . If you come this way do not forget to call in. . . . My wife died a year ago. We had been married 59 years . . . She had been ill for a couple of years and I had to feed her with a spoon . . . been writing for the Guardian over thirty years but am getting old now and will soon pack up.

He finally 'packed up' contributing to the NEATH GUARDIAN later that year on grounds of ill-health; his final column appearing on 3 December 1971. In early January 1974 Coombes was admitted to the Adelina Patti Hospital at Craig-y-Nos. He died there five months later, on 4 June 1974, at the age of eighty-one. His funeral was at St Mary's Church, Resolven, where he and Mary had been married over sixty years previously. He was buried alongside her in the church graveyard, next to the railway line he had walked along many times during the years he lived in Resolven. His coffin was draped with the flag of the St John Ambulance Association, and was accompanied by a 'Guard of Honour' made up of ambulance men. At his request, the joint gravestone was shaped as an open book, with Coombes described simply as 'Bert Lewis Coombes, Author'.

Although during the last two decades of his life Coombes had largely faded from public view, at the very end of his life a revival of interest was already underway. Only weeks after his death THESE POOR HANDS was reissued, an appreciation written by Beata Lipman (who had interviewed him in hospital just before he died) was published in PLANET (23, Summer 1974), Alun Richards included 'Twenty Tons of Coal' in his PENGUIN BOOK OF WELSH SHORT STORIES (1974) and David Smith's critical study appeared in THE ANGLO-WELSH REVIEW. On learning of some of these developments the 'Westgate' column of the WESTERN MAIL (3 July 1974) wryly remarked that *it takes death to revive interest in a long-neglected writer.*

XI

B. L. Coombes was born in England of English parents. But he spent part of his childhood, and all his adult life, living and working in Wales. He married a Welsh woman, and he learned to speak, if not to read or write, Welsh. His published work concentrated on, almost to the exclusion of everything else, the coal industry and mining communities of south Wales. But although writing, in this sense, of Wales, to what extent did Coombes see himself as a Welsh writer?

Only once did he write directly upon this issue, in replying to a questionnaire circulated by WALES magazine, and published in its edition of Autumn 1946 (6, No. 23). Asked whether he considered himself to be an *Anglo-Welsh writer*, he responded *very definitely*. Asked *Should 'Anglo-Welsh Literature' express a Welsh attitude to life and affairs, or should it merely be a literature about Welsh things?*, he answered:

It should express a Welsh attitude to life and affairs. If one writes in English the medium should be properly used – not a piebald mixture of both languages. The atmosphere and dialogue would show the Welsh attitude. Some Anglo-Welsh writers should realise that the 'shonnie-boy' period has passed and that the majority of Welsh people use the English language as it should be expressed – probably better than people of similar status in London.

Coombes's reluctance, conscious or not, to explain what he thought was meant by *a Welsh attitude to life and affairs,* was put into context by his far more direct and forthright response to the final question, *Do you believe that a sense of Welsh nationhood is more consistent with one particular attitude to life and affairs than any other?:*

> *I hardly understand this question. Certainly Welsh nationhood makes us better able to understand and love the things that are of our own nation, country, and language. Apart from that I try to have an international outlook, feeling that all mankind has rights and that good or bad can be found in all nations. To my thinking, mankind is not placed in separate compartments according to their nationality, but in two classes – drones and workers. The workers should share the honey and for the drones, I would copy the bees.*

Coombes was manifestly internationalist rather than nationalist in his outlook, but he nevertheless took a strong interest in what he considered to be 'Welsh culture'. He was a supporter of the National Eisteddfod, wanted *to see the Welsh language fostered and its use increased* (NEATH GUARDIAN, 25 August 1950), condemned those who, he felt, displayed ignorance or hostility towards it, and admired choral singing and harp music. Although most of his literary influences were American, English or Scottish, he enjoyed the prose of both Lewis Jones and Glyn Jones, and the poetry of Alun Lewis, and kept up with the contents of Welsh literary magazines such as WALES, YOUNG WALES, and the WELSH REVIEW. He was keen to see a more accurate depiction of Wales and the Welsh in literature and broadcasting, disapproving of Richard Llewellyn's HOW GREEN WAS MY VALLEY and Alexander Cordell's THE RAPE OF THE FAIR COUNTRY, and often disappointed by what he thought were the patronizing caricatures purveyed by the BBC: *I think the broadcast items should give a fairer idea of a cultured and progressive people* (NEATH GUARDIAN, 24 November 1944).

Coombes did not see Welsh culture or society as static entities. Finding a crumb of comfort in the circumstances of war, he wrote in the NEATH GUARDIAN (6 December 1940) that, given the influx of evacuees and troops that it had brought, *the ordinary people of Wales should be better known and understood than they were before*:

In these days distance is conquered by invention, and the written word is spreading swiftly across the known world. Racial barriers cannot long be maintained, and very soon we must think in terms, not of parishes, but of the whole world.

Coombes knew himself to be part of the great demographic movements that had taken place in south Wales. Writing in MINERS DAY of the cosmopolitan work-force attracted by the coal industry, he exclaimed:

What a mixture of humanity is the average mine! We have the Welsh and English language merging and being used alternately, or sometimes half and half. Their nationals never quarrel about their separate languages. Also we have some Italians working with us. They have been in this country for many years and are good men and fine workers. War has not lessened our friendship with them. Also we have a Pole and have known American miners, French miners, Belgian miners. All have worked amicably alongside me: men who have started at most of the trades in the country, and who speak in most of the dialects this land has created. Yet gradually their work here nurtures in them two dominant features – the comradeship of men who live their dangerous lives together and loyalty to their great union.

Coombes never hinted that this ethnic mixture had given rise to any social problems. On the contrary, in his article 'The Vale of Neath' in GEOGRAPHICAL MAGAZINE (15, No. 11, March 1943) he commented:

in this valley the two languages, Welsh and English, are used and the people mingle in perfect harmony. Public notices are often in both languages and each people respects the other's culture and encourages it.

Any visitor would

find a store of pleasure in visiting an area where wealth is prodigal under the ground and beauty still remains on the surface; . . . and where the people of two nationalities mingle happily, share their grievances and their poems, and count themselves as one.

Coombes wrote with great affection of the valley he had made his home, often taking the opportunity to upbraid George Borrow for having rushed through it without sufficient appreciation on his way to Merthyr Tydfil. But his greatest praise was reserved for the people of the area, who, he felt, had forged a unique culture and camaraderie that provided at least some compensation for the harsh conditions of the industry that had drawn them there. Reflecting, in THE LIFE WE WANT, on his migration from Herefordshire to south Wales, he wrote:

It was indeed a new life that I found here, and a grand comrade-ship. Some may say it is too sweeping a statement, but I am sure a larger percentage of worth-while men and women are to be found in the mining valleys than in any other areas in our land. There was no limit to their great longing to live fully, and their efforts to meet their own needs were tremendous and inspiring.

96

B. L. Coombes, in combining an 'insider's' knowledge and passion with an 'outsider's' observational distance and perspective, expressed the essential resilience of spirit and the human agency of the cosmopolitan communities of the South Wales Coalfield.

XII

I started out to write simply and directly believing that, as in music, that way is best and my placing in THE LITERATURE OF ENGLAND *seems to show that I succeeded. I liked the mining folk and their ways and have let a vast audience know it. Possibly I have been rather silent to their faults but that was an antidote to their many detractors.*

(NEATH GUARDIAN, 27 September 1963)

Bert Coombes often referred to his delight at being mentioned in William J. Entwistle and Eric Gillet's THE LITERATURE OF ENGLAND (1942 and subsequent editions), a work which listed him, on the strength of THESE POOR HANDS, as one of the most prominent autobiographers of the twentieth century. That achievement itself testifies to the stature which his writing enjoyed in some quarters, but to Coombes this was also proof that his evangelistic efforts to make known the qualities and struggles of the mining population had had some success. It is perhaps inevitable that, given its powerful impact, Coombes is primarily – often solely – remembered as the author of THESE POOR HANDS. Yet it needs emphasizing that this particular work is but a fraction of the large body of writing he penned (in 1947 he estimated he had written two million words since becoming a writer). The size of his output is even more impressive if one considers his underground work, domestic commitments and the relatively short span of his writing career (about twenty-five of his eighty-one years if his post-1960 columns for the NEATH GUARDIAN are discounted).

Coombes has not attracted a great deal of critical attention. Possibly for some, he has been regarded as insufficiently 'Welsh', although such a view must rely more on a narrow and exclusive understanding of nationality than on an open-minded appraisal of his own writings and beliefs. For others maybe, his 'proletarianism' is insufficiently strident, yet it was Arthur Horner, the Communist president of the South Wales Miners' Federation, who pledged to Coombes that he would *follow with great interest anything you write because I appreciate the reality which you express.* His work has appeared in literary anthologies, but it is as a source of historical evidence that Coombes has featured most prominently, particularly in studies of the South Wales Coalfield. That he should have interested historians more than literary critics is perhaps indicative of the largely factual and documentary nature of his output, and it can be argued that much of his fictional writing was simply an extension of his documentary impulses. Yet the reverse was also true. What makes Coombes's writing a significant literary achievement, and what takes it far beyond mere reportage or contemporary journalism, is his skilful application of the techniques of the imaginative writer to subject matter that was primarily factual. Coombes was a writer of no mean talent, and as THE TIMES LITERARY SUPPLEMENT put it (reviewing the reissue of THESE POOR HANDS on 26 July 1974), he *was one of the few proletarian writers of the 1930s who were impressive as writers rather than as proletarians.*

The impact of Coombes's writing owed much to his accessibility and readability. His characteristically limpid, spare, concise and modest, even matter-of-fact, writing style played an important part in this.

Rightly, reviewers and critics have praised the manner in which his simplicity of language and injections of humour charged his work with far greater power and conviction than would have been achieved had he adopted a more vindictive, angered, sentimental or embittered approach. David Smith is right in a general sense to suggest that Coombes eschews metaphor and simile and that in his writing there is *no desperate reaching for a linguistic vehicle for what is inexpressible in direct language. Coombes wants to tell it plain.* Yet, a distinct feature of Coombes's achievement, at least in his documentary writing on the mining industry, is his occasional use of down-to-earth imagery in order to explain what might be unclear to readers unfamiliar with the strange world of mining:

It may not be easy to visualise a coal seam so I suggest you think of a mountain as a loaf of bread which has been sliced for sandwiches. At intervals the layers of meat are placed – that's roughly how the coal seams are found. Then we'll have the miners like ants nibbling at the edge of the meat, and to stop the bread falling on them they place match sticks between the slice of bread where the meat has been taken away.

(THOSE CLOUDED HILLS)

Such writing cannot be regarded as being exceptionally fine or sophisticated, and serves to emphasize that Coombes was not a writer of outstanding innate talent. Nevertheless he had a genuine gift for explaining the unknown to his readers by using everyday language and referring to everyday things. Given that his primary aim was to be a communicator, even an educator, these devices, along with the clarity of his prose, represented a fruitful marriage of style and purpose in his writing.

Any attempt at evaluating Coombes as a writer must also assess the strong links that existed between his writing and his life. Much of his work was overtly autobiographically driven, often transparently so. His day-to-day life was a rich and plentiful source of material, which Coombes's powers of observation, eye for detail and ear for humour exploited to the full. Yet it was his experiences – and those of the mining people he lived and worked with – that were at the core of his inspiration as a writer. It is this 'lived' characteristic of his writing that gave his best work its vibrancy.

At the same time, it needs to be acknowledged that the autobiographical dimension to Coombes's writing, and his reliance on mining themes, exposed some of his limitations as a writer. When he moved beyond his own lived world of mining communities, of hill farmers and of the violin, his writing faltered and it is evident that Coombes lacked the creative power to imagine experiences, thoughts and feelings to which he himself had not been witness. This is particularly true of his efforts to write fiction. Stories such as 'The Flame', 'Machine Man' and 'Twenty Tons of Coal' are undoubtedly outstanding, and a handful of other published and unpublished ones are commendable efforts. However, given the limitations under which he laboured, it must remain doubtful whether Coombes, even if he had devoted more time to writing novels and short stories, would have achieved either critical or popular success in these genres.

If Coombes's own life was an essential influence on his writing then so too was the time in which he lived. His social, cultural, political and industrial

context is of paramount importance in understanding his writing, impact and significance. Most of his works were spontaneous responses to current events, conditions and attitudes, and this is as true of his four books as it is of the countless, almost knee-jerk, ripostes he wrote to newspapers and magazines to correct commentators who, in his eyes, made erroneous public statements about mining. His self-appointed role as the guardian of the 'truth' about the mining industry and mining communities was the springboard for his role as a public figure in wartime Britain. This in turn further encouraged him to engage in contemporary debate rather than retreat in order to write works of greater length.

Yet his significance as a writer goes far beyond his contemporary relevance. As David Smith has argued, Coombes was writing for an audience that was receptive to the nature and content of his work, though, in terms of Coombes's own trajectory as a writer, perhaps coincidentally so. During the late 1930s and the war years, in a political and intellectual climate which was grappling with the seemingly inexorable rise of Fascism, global conflict, unemployment, poverty and social decay, the sort of documentary 'truth' in which Coombes specialized found its targets. Coombes's writing articulated the social and economic injustice of contemporary capitalism and its dissipation of human talent, resources and lives; it also encapsulated the demand for a fairer and more humane society. As a proletarian who succeeded in marrying the gift of clear expression with the stamp of authenticity, Coombes functioned, as Smith suggests, as a bridge of understanding between the sympathetic and the object of their sympathy. His literary interventions (and to a lesser extent his broadcasts and films) were not merely reflective of a prevailing mood but actively influential in helping to shape events. Lehmann believed that Coombes's writing

may have had much to do with the great stirring of national conscience which eventually made the nationalization of the mines a priority no party could withstand.

(THE WHISPERING GALLERY)

This made him *most significant of the moment in English* [sic] *history in which he lived.*

Yet it would be an injustice to Coombes's writing if its importance was located only in the late 1930s and 1940s and confined to his 'moment' of acute contemporary relevance. Though he drifted out of the public gaze from the 1950s onwards, his writing has a timeless quality which is not restricted to a particular period. Partly this is because he speaks not only for the people of the South Wales Coalfield, but for miners and their families everywhere. As G. Illtyd Lewis remarked in his review of THOSE CLOUDED HILLS in WALES, 4, No. 6 (Winter 1945):

More than any other of the growing number of miner-authors he succeeds in bringing that elusive thing called 'atmosphere' to the reader. In this he is distinct from Jack Jones and Rhys Davies, who manage to produce the stuff of romance out of the Valleys without interpreting what the underground means, with its dangers, hardships and fascinations to those who by pride of vocation as well as economic necessity find themselves 'down the pit' or 'in the levels'.

Coombes's everlasting achievement is that he succeeds, arguably more effectively than any other comparable writer, in making a mass audience vividly aware of the sheer humanity as well as the inhumanity of the world of mining. His accomplishment in this respect alone makes him not just an important Welsh writer but one of British and even international significance (as those reviewers and editors from numerous countries recognized by commenting on his work and seeking contributions for their publications). Paul Lester ('By These Poor Hands: The Writings of B. L. Coombes', LONDON MAGAZINE, 33, Nos. 9–10, 1993–4) has gone further in suggesting that, apart from their obvious documentary and historical value (and, it may be suggested, a real if limited literary merit), Coombes's writings have enduring value because *they give imaginative expression to the belief that working people should have greater control of their own well-being and destiny*. Cliff John, the long-serving editor of the NEATH GUARDIAN, believed that B. L. Coombes *sent the message of the miner around the world* (27 September 1963). It is a message that still resonates.

Select Bibliography
(with Christopher Baggs)

This bibliography includes the most important known works by B. L. Coombes, plus references to selected works from the B. L. Coombes archive in the South Wales Coalfield Archive, University of Wales Swansea. It does not include Coombes's miscellaneous reviews, nor any of the material he claimed to have published in a range of journals and magazines, including BRITISH ALLY, BRITISH DIGEST and READER'S DIGEST, and in newspapers overseas. It should be noted that the bulk of Coombes's journalistic output can be found in the NEATH GUARDIAN (1940–1, 1944–71).

Books and Pamphlets

I AM A MINER, Fact No. 23, London, National Labour Press Ltd., February 1939.

THESE POOR HANDS: THE AUTOBIOGRAPHY OF A MINER WORKING IN SOUTH WALES, London, Victor Gollancz Ltd., 1939. Second edition 1974, Gollancz, with foreword by James Griffiths.

THOSE CLOUDED HILLS, London and New York, Cobbett Publishing Company, 1944.

THE LIFE WE WANT, with Rt. Hon. Lord Meston, London, Lund Humphries, 1944.

MINERS DAY, Harmondsworth and New York, Penguin, 1945.

Short Stories

'The Flame', NEW WRITING, 3, Spring 1937. Also reproduced in PENGUIN NEW WRITING, 4, 1941.

'Better Off', LEFT REVIEW, 3, No. 14, March 1938.

'Machine Man', NEW WRITING, 5, Spring 1938. Also reproduced in ARGOSY, 2, No. 16, May 1941.

'Twenty Tons of Coal', NEW WRITING (new series), 3 (Christmas 1939). Also reproduced in PENGUIN NEW WRITING, 9, September 1941, THE PENGUIN BOOK OF WELSH SHORT STORIES, ed. Alun Richards, London, Penguin, 1974, and COAL: AN ANTHOLOGY OF MINING, ed. Tony Curtis, Bridgend, Poetry Wales Press, 1997.

'Sabbath Night', FOLIOS OF NEW WRITING, 2, Autumn 1940.

OLD VICTOR, published by the Pit Ponies Protection Society (c.1942).

'Thick Candles', PENGUIN NEW WRITING, 21, 1944.

'The Problem', COAL, 3, No. 5, September 1949.

'Bitter Mischief', COAL, 4, No. 1, May 1950.

'The Opening Door', COAL, 4, No. 6, October 1950.

'One Touch', COAL, 4, No. 11, March 1951.

Articles

'Distressed', WELSH LABOUR OUTLOOK, 1, No. 2, January 1935.

'What Life Means to Me', LEFT REVIEW, December 1936.

'Colliery Ambulance Man', DAILY HERALD, 7 April 1937.

'Can We Have Educated Slaves?', REYNOLDS NEWS, 29 August 1937.

[as 'Glamorgan'] 'From Darkness – into the Light', HEALTH AND EFFICIENCY, 7, August 1937.

'This is the Problem', PICTURE POST, 10, No. 1, 4 January 1941.

'Mining Accidents and Disease', FORTNIGHTLY, 149, January 1941.

'The Way We Live Now – I', PENGUIN NEW WRITING, 2, January 1941.

'Below the Tower', FOLIOS OF NEW WRITING, 3, Spring 1941.

'A Sheep Gets Rescued', PICTURE POST, 14, No. 8, 21 February 1942.

'Points of View: I. The Miner', FORTNIGHTLY, 151, March 1942.

'A Miner's Record – I', NEW WRITING AND DAYLIGHT, Summer 1942.

'Craftsman or Robot?', THE LISTENER, 28, No. 716, 1 October 1942.

'A Miner's Record – II', NEW WRITING AND DAYLIGHT, Winter 1942/3.

'The Boy in the Mine', FORTNIGHTLY, 153, March 1943.

'The Vale of Neath', GEOGRAPHICAL MAGAZINE, 15, No. 11, March 1943.

'A Miner's Record – III', NEW WRITING AND DAYLIGHT, Summer 1943.

'The Miner's Life in Wartime', PICTURE POST, 21, No. 5, 30 October 1943.

'Joint Control in Mining', FORTNIGHTLY, 155, February 1944.

'Dusty Retort', NEW STATESMAN AND NATION, 10 June 1944.

'Bevin Boys at Work', GEOGRAPHICAL MAGAZINE, 17, No. 6, October 1944.

'Mr Foot tells the coal-owners: and a coal-miner tells Mr Foot', PICTURE POST, 26, No. 8, 24 February 1945.

'The Miner and the Machine', FORTNIGHTLY, 158, August 1945.

'Singing Wood', GEOGRAPHICAL MAGAZINE, 18, No. 6, October 1945.

'The Miner and Nationalization', FORTNIGHTLY, 951, March 1946.

'Their Hour has Struck', DAILY WORKER, 2 January 1947.

'Valley of Wales', ANVIL: LIFE AND THE ARTS, ed. Jack Lindsay, London, Meridian Books, 1947.

'The Vale of Neath', WALES, 7, No. 25, Spring 1947.

'A Bob a Day: How Much is a Miner's Experience Worth?', DAILY WORKER, 7 May 1947.

'You are being Watched', COAL, 1, No. 4, August 1947.

'And Now – the First Year of Nationalisation in South Wales is Summed Up', COAL, 1, No. 9, January 1948.

'Pit Parliament', COAL, 1, No. 12, April 1948.

'The Eight-Pointed Star', COAL, 2, No. 2, June 1948.

'A Farm on your Doorstep', COAL, 2, No. 5, September 1948.

'Hats Off to the Man Behind the Seams', COAL, 3, No. 2, June 1949.

'A Miner Considers', FORTNIGHTLY, 1013, May 1951.

'The Mines To-Day', FORTNIGHTLY, 1042, October 1953.

'The Lights of Love', DAILY MIRROR, 29 April 1955.

Miscellaneous
Replies to Wales questionnaire, WALES, 6, No. 23, Autumn 1946.

Letter of congratulations, WALES, 7, No. 26, Summer 1947.

Radio documentaries: held both in the National Library of Wales and the BBC Written Archives Centre, Reading. See 'Bitter Idleness' (1943), 'Back to the Land' (1943), and 'The Working-Class Writer' (1947) in WALES ON THE WIRELESS: A BROADCASTING ANTHOLOGY, ed. Patrick Hannan, Llandysul, Gomer, 1988.

Unpublished Material Mentioned in the Text
[located in South Wales Coalfield Archive]

'Castell Vale', *c*.1935.

'The War Diary of a Welsh Miner', 1939–1941.

'I Stayed a Miner' [radio play], 1957.

'Home on the Hill: An Autobiography', 1959.

'The Singing Sycamore' [n.d.].

Mary Coombes, 'My Life from Childhood' [n.d.].

FACE OF COAL: A PROVOCATIVE DOCUMENTARY [stage play] with Jack Lindsay, 1946 [located in the National Library of Australia].

'Scrapbook' [n.d.].

Note: for a description of the archive's holdings see Bill Jones and Chris Williams, 'The B. L. Coombes Archive', WELSH WRITING IN ENGLISH, 5 (1999). Extracts from 'Castell Vale', 'The War Diary' and 'Home on the Hill' appear, along with some previously unpublished short stories, in Bill Jones and Chris Williams (eds.), WITH DUST STILL IN HIS THROAT: A B. L. COOMBES ANTHOLOGY (Cardiff, University of Wales Press, 1999).

Critical Literature

Christopher M. Baggs, 'A "war-time mirror to Welsh life"? B. L. Coombes and the *Neath Guardian*', MORGANNWG, 34 (1990).

Jenni Calder, CHRONICLES OF CONSCIENCE: A STUDY OF GEORGE ORWELL AND ARTHUR KOESTLER, London, Secker & Warburg, 1968.

'Coombes, Bert Lewis', in DICTIONARY OF LABOUR BIOGRAPHY, Vol. 4, ed. Joyce M. Bellamy and John Saville, London and Basingstoke, Macmillan, 1977.

Andy Croft, 'Major miner writers and the British Left between the Wars', WORKING-CLASS LITERATURE IN BRITAIN AND IRELAND IN THE NINETEENTH AND TWENTIETH CENTURIES, Part I, Humboldt, 1985.

Paul Lester, 'By These Poor Hands: the writings of B. L. Coombes', LONDON MAGAZINE, 33, Nos. 9–10, 1993–4.

Beata Lipman, 'Bert Coombes', PLANET, 23, Summer 1974.

Philip Norman, 'The Boy who Escaped from the Valley of Witches', THE TIMES, 29 December 1979.

Ramon Lopez Ortega, LA CRISIS ECONOMICA DE 1929 Y LA NOVELISTICA DE TEMA OBRERO EN GRAN BRETAÑA EN LOS AÑOS TREINTA, Salamanca, 1974.

David Smith, 'Underground man: the work of B. L. Coombes, "miner writer"', THE ANGLO-WELSH REVIEW, 24, No. 53, Winter 1974.

Acknowledgements

The authors would like to thank the following individuals for their generous assistance and support in the preparation of this work: Chris Baggs, Elisabeth Bennett, Tony Brown, Janet Davies, Vivian Davies, Brian Dyson, Susan Jenkins, Ceinwen Jones, R. Brinley Jones, Stephen Knight, Susan Knowles, Siân Moran, Liz Powell, Alun Richards, John Saville, Peter Stead, Meic Stephens, David Thomas, Ned Thomas, Ceri Thompson and Christine Woodland.

They would also like to record their appreciation for the help of staff at the British Library, the British Library Document Supply Centre, the British Library Newspaper Library, the Brynmor Jones Library at the University of Hull, Cardiff Central Library, Cardiff University Library, the Glamorgan Record Office, the Herefordshire Record Office, the National Library of Wales, Neath Public Library, Sussex University Library and University of Wales Swansea Library.

The Authors

Bill Jones is originally from Llandeilo and gained his first degree and doctorate at University College, Cardiff. Between 1982 and 1993 he was a Research Assistant then Assistant Keeper with responsibility for coal mining collections at the National Museum of Wales. Since 1994 he has been a Lecturer in Modern Welsh History at the School of History and Archaeology, Cardiff University. He is the author of *Wales in America: Scranton and the Welsh, 1860–1920* and *Teyrnas Y Glo / Coal's Domain: Historical Glimpses of the South Wales Coalfield* (with Beth Thomas), as well as various other publications on Welsh emigration and Welsh communities outside Wales, and the industrial, social and cultural history of the South Wales Coalfield during the nineteenth and twentieth centuries.

Chris Williams was born in Griffithstown, Monmouthshire, in 1963. He was educated at Churchfields Comprehensive School, Swindon, Wiltshire and at the Royal Military Academy, Sandhurst. After reading History at Balliol College, Oxford, he researched for a Ph.D. on the political history of the Rhondda Valleys at University College, Cardiff. He has lectured in British and Welsh History at Cardiff University since 1988. He has published numerous articles and essays on the political and social history of Wales and Britain and is author of both *Democratic Rhondda: Politics and*

Society, 1885–1951 (1996) and *Capitalism, Community and Conflict: The South Wales Coalfield, 1898–1947* (1998). From 1990 to 1994 he was secretary of Llafur: The Welsh Labour History Society.

Designed by Jeff Clements
Typesetting at the University of Wales Press in
11pt Palatino and printed in Great Britain by
Dinefwr Press, Llandybïe, 1999

British Library Cataloguing in Publication Data.
A catalogue record for this book is available from the
British Library.

ISBN 0-7083-1562-3

The Publishers wish to acknowledge the financial
assistance of the Arts Council of Wales towards the cost
of producing this volume.